A little about **Gardening for Disabled Trust**

In 1968, Mrs Peggy Kinsey created the Gardening for Disabled Trust. A prescient and inspired lady, she observed that being outside in the fresh air, doing a little gardening and getting the 'soil under the fingernails' was helpful to well-being. Half a century later, the value of 'horticultural therapy' is well-known; and the Gardening for Disabled Trust continues to award grants to those facing all kinds of mental and physical challenges, helping them defy their disabilities and making gardening possible again. Our clients tell us that these little grants can be 'life-changing'. Thank you for supporting the Trust, and helping more people re-discover the pleasure of gardening.

Gardenir
Disabled

GW00500371

FOREWORD

Good gardeners are not selfish; heavens no! They are fired with missionary zeal when it comes to passing on hints and tips to others who want to green up their patch of land and to enjoy the experience. It's a passion that is infectious, and those who have contributed to this little book prove as much. I have long been an enthusiastic supporter of 'Gardening for Disabled Trust' – an organisation which believes passionately that everyone should be able to enjoy a garden regardless of physical disadvantage. You'll find within these pages advice from great gardeners as well as people whose names are familiar but who might surprise you with their knowledge and their interest. By having a copy of your own, you, too will be doing your bit to spread the word and support an organisation whose valuable work deserves to be celebrated.

Enjoy the book – and your garden!

ALAN TITCHMARSH, MBE

Contents

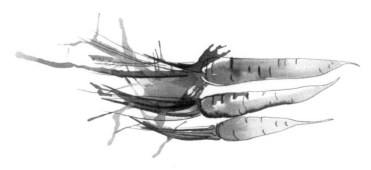

Case Study; how a grant from GDT helped a community

Stanley Grange is a small sheltered residential community set in rural Lancashire providing homes for adults with learning disabilities, many of whose families and financing local authorities come from all over the UK.

It is a vibrant happy place with small scale housing which can cater for up to 42 people, all arranged around a central village green and a community hall for social activities.

Stanley Grange is working hard to develop services that provide opportunities for employment, education, training and volunteering. This includes a thriving garden centre that is being upgraded after many years of neglect. Fifteen of the residents currently work here, propagating, caring and nurturing a good selection of plants, which are for sale to general public, along with hanging baskets and Christmas Wreaths. Willow is grown to make sculptures, and wooden planters are also made.

GDT were delighted to provide a grant that enabled the purchase of 4 sturdy trolleys with which to transport plants, soil and general gardening equipment around the nursery. Trustee David Bell was extremely grateful and said "Being able to purchase the trolleys will be a tremendous help and make such a difference as they are items that we have needed for some time".

One of the GDT committee members was able to pay Stanley Grange a visit over the summer and was delighted to meet several residents, including Mark, whose passion, (amongst a few others!) is growing vegetables. He said the trolleys were light, manoeuvrable and incredibly useful.

1. DESIGN PRINCIPLES & PRACTICALITIES

GARDEN DESIGN

Gardens are private worlds. Their edges define them; whether they gaze out or cocoon in. Walls, hedges or ha-has set the bounds, character and spirit of the garden and its relationship with the world outside. *Kim Wilkie, Garden Designer*

Get a feel for the spirit and soul of your garden.
Kate Ball, Kate Ball Garden Design

Every garden should have a vista or two: long and narrow openings through which a view or object of beauty can be glimpsed. Particularly in smaller gardens, this view can be of a spectacular tree or plant or best of all, a sculpture. *Cameron Foye, Sculptor*

Keep it simple! I like to design gardens with subtle hard landscaping and then allow the planting to 'soften' everything, with its billows and curves. *Kate Ball*

Remember that scale, proportion and balance are the main criteria, think of mass and void. When we go into a new garden we read the void, that is the space that is left behind and it is the mass that defines the space. *Sarah Eberle, Landscape Designer*

A well-known phrase in garden design is 'the borrowed landscape'. This is key and means absorbing and appreciating the surrounding landscape. You may be lucky enough to have country views. If you are amongst other houses, they may have mature trees which can enhance your outlook. *Kate Ball*

Easy Style Wins

Don't mix too many types of plants – stick to one or two for a better effect. I always have lots of pink geraniums and a few lavenders. Nothing else. *Julian Clary*

Plant a small, slow growing tree in a large pot and you have instant maturity to a new patio or garden. Acers are fantastic examples of trees that do really well in confined conditions and add lots of interest and style to your space. Leafy flowering plants are also another great option – bananas and cannas in particular are great at adding height, interest and a touch of glam. If you love the cottage garden look combine fruit with flowers. It's a winner. If you are short on space, espalier and cordon trees are a great way to introduce fruit to walls and fences. *Liz Ridgway, www.denysandfielding.co.uk*

Layout and creating a garden for all the seasons

Ensure that the layout flows well from the house and there is enough space in each area to serve its purpose, e.g. ramp distances, wheelchair accessibility and ease of movement; surfaces that are appropriate for use, e.g. non-slip etc. Look at materials you are considering and get a sample to check they will meet your requirements, colour, size etc. When creating a plant list, consider texture, colour, feel, fragrance and full-grown size as well as ongoing maintenance. Create a plant list that will tolerate your site conditions and fill your requirements. Make a story board of your final overall ideas and plant list to get a good idea of what the space will look like before you begin. *Jo Connolly, Jo Connolly Design*

Start the garden layout plan with the winter season. It is easy to fill up a garden in summer but it is how the garden looks in winter that is also important – you still want to look at something good in the garden then. *Christina Carter*

Remember when trying to incorporate all-year-round interest that should not mean it is the same all year round! Seasonal change is to be celebrated and foliage, bark and shape are as important as flowers. In general, keep winter, spring and autumn colour closer to the house and summer interest further into the garden. It is more likely you will be using the garden in the outer regions in the summer and if not in the forefront of the view from the house then the winter die-back is not in the immediate picture.
Sarah Eberle, Landscape Designer

Shrubs

Shrubs should be the skeleton of a garden. The perennials can then grow around them to flesh out the rest. Having a mixture of shrubs that flower at different seasons means you have interest throughout the year. *@Generous Gardener*

Shape your shrubs and trees – snipping away to reveal trunks and stems is a really easy way to make a garden look well-kept and interesting. It also provides a little more air and space in and around ground level, often making it easier to establish a weave of low-growing ground-covering plants. *Liz Ridgway*

Keep an eye out for interesting and sculptural tree roots, rocks, pieces of scrap or unusual containers. Properly placed these can add full stops or pivots to flowerbeds or vistas bringing interest and excitement to a garden. *Cameron Foye, Sculptor*

PRACTICALITIES

When planning your garden give some thought to one or two extra seating areas where you can enjoy a different aspect or vista to the one you see from your main patio. It's always good to create a sunny and sheltered area to relax in throughout the year, especially if you have a shady north-facing plot. *Alison Moore, Manchester*

Build a ground water feature. This could be an old washing-up bowl with a few rocks in but you will be amazed how quickly it becomes a whole new world of life and this will benefit your garden enormously including pest control. *Philip Bailey*

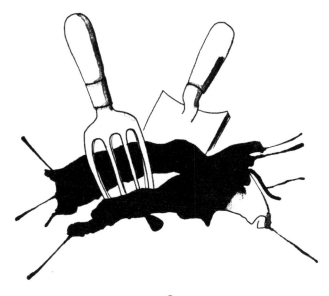

Think of how you want to use the space, for example, 'entertainment for 4 people', 'BBQ and cooking area', 'access to wheelie bins', 'herbs for the whole year'. This should dictate the layout and arrangement of your space, thereafter plan your features and plants. *Jason Peters*

If you can get a hammock in there, do, it's a good way to relax and great for star gazing. *Martha Krempel, Martha Krempel Garden Design*

When developing a garden, however small, it is always good to repeat the same plant on the diagonal. That way it leads the eye down the garden, extends a small space or unites a larger one. I always plant in odd numbers, i.e. 3's for a small garden and more for larger ones. *Alice Coptcoat*

Don't forget foliage plants to give variety of colour, structure and texture in your garden. It can be what keeps winter interest too in your garden. Add some lighter or variegated foliage in shady beds as they will lift the area and create a colour pop and contrast. *Hilary O'Donnell Cam*

When choosing a tree for your garden be sure to check the height and spread when it is fully grown. Give the tree plenty of room for its eventual size so you can enjoy it in all its glory. Cherry trees are a great choice for small to medium sized gardens, have multi-season interest with fabulous blossom in spring and many have lovely autumn colour. *Joe Archer, Gardener at Hole Park Garden*

I love having evergreen in the garden, from trees to hedges, they provide real structure to any garden and add colour all year round. *Sophie Allport, www.sophieallport.com*

Don't have too many evergreen shrubs - mix them up with deciduous otherwise it is too heavy. *Christina Carter*

As a newcomer to gardening I come from the "make it up as you go along" school of thought. So I bought collections of perennials on line. Not the small plugs but the ready to plant plants. Don't plant in lines, go for clusters of 3. Mix in a few Allium bulbs too. Buy a few well-established hero plants as your eye goes straight to them rather than that row of slightly boring bushes. I bought a banana tree and it's not only the thrill of the beautiful leaves unfolding throughout the Summer but the baby off shoots pop up too. They are called pups. *Jim Henderson*

Start Small! *Lance French*

Be wary of mixing too many variegated shrubs together. Keep an eye open for shrub reverting to plain from variegated. *Christina Carter*

To see ambitious, head-height planting is a joy; it draws the eye, adds texture, romance and can be achieved no matter how small your garden. *Claire Saxby*

Trees in urban environments: Many trees are tolerant of pollution. Hornbeam (*Carpinus betulus*) trees are especially useful as they survive in areas where pollution levels are high, making hornbeams the perfect choice of tree for an urban environment. *Acer campestre, Alnus glutinosa, Corylus avellana 'Aurea', Mespilus germanica*, and *Taxus baccata* are other tree options for city gardens. *Beth Otway, Horticulturist and Garden Writer*

Stimulate the senses to restore your mind, body and soul.

Select plants that stir emotions and stimulate all the senses so as to restore the mind. For sight, use highly saturated bright colours such as true blue forget-me-nots, *Myosotis sylvatica* and bright yellows for joy by growing sunflowers *Helianthus annuus*. Incorporate plants with fractals such as the soft shield fern *Polystichum setiferum* (Divisilobum Group) 'Herrenhausen' to restore the mind. For sound, encourage birds into your garden especially the restorative sounds of the Dunnock, Greenfinch and Blackbird. For touch, choose soft to touch plants such as grasses and lambs ear (*Stachys byzantina*). For scent fill your spaces with scent of Lavender *Lavandula angustifolia* which physiologically relaxes you or plants that smell of chocolate such as *Cosmos atrosanguineus* 'Chocamocha' and *Azara microphylla variegata* or that smell of candyfloss, such as the candyfloss tree *Cercidiphyllum japonicum* 'Boyd's Dwarf'. For taste stimulate with chilli peppers, hot to taste and touch or the cooling effects of mint. Enjoy growing, seeing, tasting, smelling, touching and eating delicious strawberries. *Prof Alistair Griffiths, Director of Science and Collections of the RHS & co-author of 'RHS Your Wellbeing Garden'*

Plant scented repeat flowering roses and you'll have a bloom for most days of the year. Get a tree into your garden – there is always a specimen to suit in size texture or colour. *Martha Krempel*

Too many scents in a garden can overpower the senses & be too much for us to take in. Think of key points around your garden where you might want scents. The main routes, the front or back door, where you sit, which part of the garden gets sun and whether you want scent in the evening as well as the day. This is great for the visually-impaired as the scented plants can become markers within the space. Don't forget scent comes from flowers, leaves & the oils so mix it up. *Mark Lane, Writer, Broadcaster, Garden Designer*

The client brief is vital when designing a garden, as every brief is unique. So before you search for a designer, make sure you have really thought about what you would like from your new garden, do some research and write a wish list. When deciding on a designer, ensure whoever you choose you really like as a person, as it's so important to get on and communicate with each other throughout the design process. It can be a fabulous journey. *Raine Clarke-Wills, Raine Garden Design*

Ask yourself 'What do you want?' and 'What have you got?' Make a checklist of everything you might need from a patio to a greenhouse and everything in between. Next really look around you and if the garden is already established take a year to see just what comes up and get a real feeling of what you have. Where does the sun swing throughout the day for sun and shade, what soil do you have (check it with a simple kit), good or bad views, slopes, boundaries, prevailing winds. Any trees next door that overshadow your plot and take goodness from your soil. Make a simple scale plan on graph paper and start to rough the areas out. Crisp and neat close to the house and softer and looser further away to create a real feeling of space and movement. To see how it will look, peg out the shape of a lawn, the line of a generous path and the position of beds, some of which could be raised, ensuring ease of access and cultivation Place stakes for tree positions. Wait for as long as you need and if necessary adjust things until you are absolutely happy. Now and only now is it time to start work, how exciting! *David Stevens, David Stevens International*

Designing an easier-to-manage garden:

Access is the number one priority for wheelchairs, and narrow raised beds so that you can reach to do all your own deadheading (the single most satisfying job of the summer). I use my kitchen grabber or a walking stick in my feeble hand, to pull stems towards me, and then snip with the secateurs in my right hand. *Melanie Reid, Writer, The Times*

Find what you can do from patios and paths: and for planting, think about the levels. If like me, you are in a wheelchair then it's raised beds and borders and ways to get alongside pots and tubs. We replanted some pots at the nursing home with 'Hidcote' Lavender and they have grown into nicely shaped balls, giving a clean look to our decking area. Alstroemerias, Peruvian lilies – a perennial – have given us much pleasure with many different colours to choose from and they flower all summer: they're very easy to grow and look good, simply prune them to ground level in the autumn. *Jeremy Homewood, Bumbles Plant Centre*

Whilst caring for mum, as she is unable to be active in her garden, I included her in planting seeds in pots in the house for the greenhouse. Also moved pots to her height on a table, to dead head pansies. Involving her is so important. Growing vegetables in her greenhouse has brought her lots of pleasure. Funny thing, at bedtime, she has reminded us to water her runner beans, in her mind her garden is still being tended by her. *Gill Keenor*

Toiling in the garden in one's twilight years is not a joy for everyone. Plan ahead: keep it small and simple and get lots of help. *Michael Rudman DL.*

If you have less time available and everything you do takes longer now, you may want to reduce the time spent maintaining your garden. You could simplify your garden by:

A. Growing low-maintenance perennial plants and shrubs rather than growing annuals from seed. Or at least buy seedlings or young plants rather than grow from seed.

B. Turning large flower beds into lawn. We also converted some very narrow flowerbeds into gravel strips (mostly by the house or fence) and kept the existing raised beds. We made the front garden flowerbeds smaller by extending the drive as well as by planting a variety of deciduous and evergreen shrubs and trees.

C. Surrounding shrubs and trees with a thick layer of bark mulch (2-3in) also keeps beds moist and helps to keep down weeds, thereby saving time on watering and weeding.

D. Installing a sturdy obelisk by the steps so that you have something to hold onto when climbing up or down. You can then grow a decorative climber through it such as a rose, clematis or passionflower. *Andrea Ballard*

Build a raised vegetable plot with sufficient space all round to get a wheelbarrow or wheelchair. Make it narrow enough so that you can reach over to tend the plot. *Allan Pemberton*

Generally better to avoid gnomes! *Sue Rowles*

For garden with all year round interest, go to the garden centre once a month and buy something that's in flower. *@aradgick*

Low Maintenance Lawns

Why not plant a flowering lawn, using naturally low growing plants like thyme (*Thymus*), daisies (*Bellis perennis*), clover (*Trifolium*), thrift (*Armeria maritima*), and birds foot trefoil (*Lotus corniculatus*)? These plants will flourish in a sunny or partially shaded site with well-drained soil. If you'd prefer a green lawn, why not create a blissfully relaxing space using scented chamomile (*Chamaemelum nobile*)? Chamomile grows best in well-drained soils, in bright and sunny areas. If your garden is shaded or damp underfoot, why not think about cultivating a smooth velvety carpet of moss. *Beth Otway*

The only thing that connects us to the outside is the garden of our house. This may not be a problem for those who live alone or who love city life, but for families and especially families with children, even if it is tiny, the garden has an important value. A minimalist, simple, functional and sustainable garden, no more is needed to be happy. *Ata Polat, Landscape Architect*

2. SOWING & SCATTERING, CUTTING & PROPOPGATING

SOWING & SCATTERING, CUTTING & PROPOGATING

SOWING SEEDS

Sowing lots of annuals is a great way to give you an 'instant garden' feel, while your shrubs, trees and perennials get going. Sow lots of bee friendly plants like borage, sunflowers and scabious, the bees and butterflies will flock to them. *Lisbet Rausing, Nicky Browne, Head Gardener at Wadhurst Park and Sara Jackson, Gardener at Rolf's Farm.*

Some of the most exotic plants can be grown from the seed of fruits and vegetables you buy on your weekly shop. I've grown pomegranate from seed of a fruit bought at my local supermarket and in my sheltered garden it flourishes in a planter. (You should never bring seeds into the UK from overseas as you can introduce diseases to our own flora and fauna). *Andrew Fisher Tomlin, Fisher Tomlin & Bowyer Garden Designers*

If you have a greenhouse, conservatory or just a sunny windowsill, it's worth filling trays with seeds of high summer annuals, such as cosmos, tithonia and snapdragons, in late April and May. They can then be planted out in June, once any danger of frost is past. *Vanessa Berridge*

Lengths of plastic guttering filled with compost make perfect starter beds for all manner of seedlings and can be slid straight into the ground when the time comes. They use less compost than individual pots and allow compact sowing and growing. *Simon Lycett, Celebrity Floral Designer*

Too many seedlings germinated? Share them with friends and family!
@ Generous Gardener

…Or become the modern-day Ellen Willmott who used to scatter
seeds of her favourite plant *Eryngium giganteum* in friends' gardens;
Eryngium giganteum is now known as 'Miss Willmott's Ghost'.
Quentin Stark, Head Gardener, Hole Park

This might be one for the young gardeners… next time you eat a
really delicious tasty tomato cut a slice with lots of seeds in and pop
it in a compost tray, cover with more compost over the top, not too
deep and water. You should get a germination of little tommy
seedlings to prick out eventually. *Debbie Hobden*

Seeds need to be kept cool, stored in the dark and dry over
the winter. *Matthew Berridge, Zoo Gardener*

Sow hardy annual plants seed in September/October for an earlier
flowering and often stronger plant the following year.
Lisbet Rausing, Nicky Browne, Sara Jackson

Never give up on slow to germinate seeds. Often they take ages
more than stated on the packet and can surprise if you have a
little patience. *@Generous Gardener*

Growing from seed is exciting but obviously takes longer especially
if growing trees! Don't throw away pots of seed. Tip in a border if
they are unsuccessful and label in case they germinate at a later date.
You never know you may grow a new hybrid, dahlias from seed for
example. *Quentin Stark*

Minimize your trips to garden centres – grow as much as you can from seed and make friends with other gardeners who will share and swap plants. *Isabella Tree, Knepp Re-Wilding Project*

COLLECTING & SCATTERING

Seed Collection is an easy way to save money. To save your flowerbeds from too many self-sown seedlings collect the seeds before they fall. Flowers like cow-parsley, aquilegia, poppies & fennel can be harvested. Place a brown paper bag over the head of the flower once it has been pollinated, cut off the stem & hang upside down until all the seed has dropped in the bag. Plant again when appropriate. *Mark Lane, Writer, Broadcaster & Garden Designer*

If you are keeping seed from your own plants, only do so from individuals that are perfectly healthy and show no signs of disease; and don't bother saving seed from F1 hybrid varieties which will not come true. *Professor Stefan Buczacki*

For a 'natural' biennial forest of foxgloves: leave some old flower stems lying on the ground each autumn in a suitable site. The stems will remind you where not to weed. Zillions of tiny seedlings will germinate each spring, many will perish but just enough will survive. Thin out/transplant 1-year-old seedlings so that plants are at least 30cms apart in their second (flowering) year. *Helen Yemm, Daily Telegraph Columnist and author of 'Gardening in Pyjamas'.*

One year's seeds is seven years' wildlife haven.
Gill Burn, Northumberland

Hardy annuals such as Love-in-the-mist and little papery poppies make bigger, better plants if they self-sow and germinate in situ in the autumn. Transplant them if necessary with a good, damp clod of undisturbed soil and they may not notice the disruption.
Helen Yemm

Seedlings of perennials make better roots and therefore sturdier plants more quickly if they are not allowed to flower in their first year. *Helen Yemm*

If, like me, you grow annual flowers then it's well worthwhile saving the seeds at the end of the season. If you've not done it before, or even if you have, have a look at the The Seed Site website for lots of useful information. *@sofaflyer*

You can tell the eventual flower colour of seedlings (e.g. cosmos and hellebores) by the colour of their stems — various degrees of pink if they are going to be pink/red, or pure green if they are going to be white. In the case of foxgloves, look at the base of their leaves.
Helen Yemm

Succession planting

Grow micro-salads in greenhouse beds or boxes by sowing succession crops every few weeks. They will survive in winter quite well. Good supplier is CN seeds. *John Mankelow*

Sowing lettuce economically. Tip only enough seeds into the palm of your hand to cover a 5p piece. Sow them into a yogurt pot. Transplant when big enough and keep doing this every 2 weeks and it will keep you in lettuces through the summer, using just one packet of seeds. *Josie Matthews*

I don't find successive planting or sowing easy but doing so, with both flowers and vegetables, gives a much longer growing season. *@sofaflyer*

Tree seed germination

I have found germinating these seeds works in a clear plastic bag. Mix the seed in a 60% peat- 40% perlite and regularly mist to keep moist. Keep indoors somewhere at room temperature. Take seedlings out when germinated and pot up in 9cm pot.
Graham Smith

Sweet peas

Plant sweet pea seeds in pots in the autumn for bigger and stronger roots ready to flower in late May and early June. Once they have produced 3 pairs of leaves pinch out the tip for a bushier plant and look forward to picking wonderful bunches of sweet peas in early summer. *Melanie Todd*

If you have trouble getting your sweet pea seeds to germinate, try the following; dampen some kitchen paper and place in a shallow container or on a plate. Place the sweet pea seeds on top. Make sure that the kitchen paper does not dry out by occasionally spraying with water over the following days. Once the seeds have germinated, place the container/plate near a window. Pot up the seedlings once they are large enough to handle and plant out when frost is no longer a danger. *Adam Piper*

Agapanthus

When your agapanthus has stopped flowering cut the heads off on a long stalk. Hang upside down in a carrier bag to dry and the seeds will fall into the bag. Store them in a sealed bag until the following March/April. Sow in a seed tray, filled with gritty compost. Cover with grit or compost. Keep moist. The seeds will germinate; nurture them, potting on as they grow. In a few years, with patience, you will have a large number of new plants from a single head. *Anne F*

To get evenly spaced parsnips, sow seeds in loo rolls. Once germinated, remove all but one seedling. Plant out as soon as the root appears, at the desired spacing. *Sarah Peters*

Never give up. Sow and sow again until you find the correct time and method. Always read the packet and follow the instructions, but remember if it's too cold, wet or frozen wait until the conditions improve. *Christine Walkden, Horticulturalist*

CUTTING & PROPAGATING

You can take cuttings at almost any time throughout the year,
Summer is best of all when you can propagate from shrubs, tender
perennials like salvias and even from hardy perennials. Take shoots
about 4 inches/10cm. Trim underneath a leaf node and take off the
bottom set of leaves. Nip out the growing tip, insert cuttings up to
the bottom leaves in a clay pot containing gritty compost. Water
once and keep in a warm place but out of direct sunlight. When you
see white roots protruding from the drainage hole it's time to pot
up cuttings individually. *Carol Klein*

I've found that when taking summer, softwood cuttings of
Penstemon, that are full of sap, often the cutting starts to wilt
then continues to wilt and will not root, eventually rotting off.
The easiest way to solve this problem is to nip the growing tip out
when preparing the cutting. Not only does this solve the wilting
problem but also encourages them to send out more shoots once
rooted. *Nick Hamilton, Barnsdale Gardens*

When taking cuttings of rosemary and pelargoniums, fuchsias
and so on, dip the cut end into cider vinegar before inserting into
compost – it will act as a fungicide and keep bugs and baddies at
bay, encouraging good strong root growth. *Simon Lycett,*
Celebrity Floral Designer

SOWING & SCATTERING,
CUTTING & PROPOGATING

Grape vine cuttings:

When cutting back your grape vine in spring March/April before it starts bearing leaf. Cut 20-30cm length with 3/4 node, cut the top on an angle about 1cm away from the node. Dip bottom into rooting powder or gel, and place into heated propagator. Leave for 4/6 weeks and you should get 70/80% of them to root.
Graham Smith

Suckers from Trees:

When separating suckers to keep for replanting from trees such as *Sorbaria* or *Rhus*, sever the main underground root from the mother tree but keep the sucker in the ground for another season before removing in order for it to develop its own root system. It can then be lifted and potted on or replanted. *Shelley O'Berg, Cambo Heritage Trust*

Dahlia cuttings:

Dahlias produce more prolifically and better flowers from cuttings taken from tubers in the Spring. I double my chances by digging some of the tubers up and leaving others in the ground overwinter – covering the ones in the ground with straw, compost and ferns. Any dahlia failures (too short a vase life or not flowering profusely) I mark with a coloured label before they finish flowering to make sure I dispose of the right ones. *Sheila Hume, Kent Flower Farmer*

Rose cuttings:

Roses are easy to propagate and may flower the following year depending on when you take cuttings. I avoid the winter months. Organic home made compost is the perfect medium for growing

26

roses. Fill a 1-3L pot and tap the pot to settle the compost. The rose stem should be a little thicker than a pencil, free of pests and diseases, no flowers buds growing. 50% of the stem should be below the surface of the soil reaching the bottom of the pot and 50% above soil level. Keep soil moist with rainwater, place in a sheltered, sunny spot around 21°C. Look out for new leaves emerging. Plant out when roots fill pot and the soil is warm – ideally spring to autumn. *Sarah McLean Barr*

Rubber plant / yucca cuttings:
I've discovered that a tall straggly rubber plant or yucca can be chopped off at a suitable height to make two plants from the upper and lower parts. The lower stumpy end will produce two side shoots (as yuccas are actually sold) when planted in fresh compost, while the top end can be potted up minus its dead leaves and with the stem trimmed to a suitable length. Stand the pot in a saucer of water and it will produce roots and make a whole new plant. So two for the price of one! Yucca and rubber plants can be kept outdoors in summer. *Alison Beach*

Bulb Propagation:
I love propagating! If I have one I want six! Years ago, I bought a bulb of *Eucomis autumnalis* and was pleased to find that it could be propagated by leaf cuttings. Because the flower spike had a top like a pineapple I tried rooting that and it worked. I've never seen that in any book! Loads of tiny bulbs grow along the cut! When they're big enough, seperate them and grow them on! *Maurice Wilkins*

NOTES & OBSERVATIONS

----

3. SOIL, WEEDS & THE DARK ART OF COMPOSTING

SOIL

Treat soil like the best food you'd want to eat. Prepare it well by
adding the right nutrients and ingredients to it, to give your plants
the best chance to grow and flourish. *Hilary O'Donnell Cam,
Garden Designer*

Get the soil right and you will end up with strong roots and
happy, healthy plants! Top-mulching with organic, screened
mulch/compost in the winter is the best way. Always mulch over
wet ground to preserve the moisture and to a depth of at least
10cm. This creates essential bacteria and fungus in the soil
encouraging earthworms and suppresses weeds. Happy mulching!!
Anna Ingram, Professional Horticulturalist

Test your soil for pH balance before deciding on a planting plan and
prepare soil well prior to planting. Also look at the orientation and
ensure you position plants accordingly. *Georgina Stewart*

One no dig bed can give so much pleasure and food, without any
need for the heavy work of preparing soil for each new planting.
The surface compost is always ready for seeds and transplants, so you
keep cropping all through the season. Top up the surface with 3cm
new compost, once a year. *Charles Dowding, Author of
'No Dig Gardening'.*

We dig as little as we can in the garden to avoid disturbing the
micro-life, we feed our soil regularly with our compost, use
compost teas as foliar feeds, and grow green manures such as
phacelia and crimson clover to help the structure and life in the soil.
Henrietta Courtauld, The Land Gardeners

In my gardening lifetime soil science has advanced enormously. Forty or so years ago I learned a traditional practice of putting well-rotted manure in the bottom of tree and shrub planting holes. It was a well-intentioned but pointless activity. Spread any manures or compost as a mulch on the surface, so the goodness can go down to feed the soil and be made available to roots. *Richard Huggett*

Nourish the ground in the Autumn with well-rotted manure and/or green manures, such as Field Beans and Hairy Vetch. *Kevin Fortey, 3 times Guinness World Record Holder and current record holder for the World's Heaviest Beetroot weighing 23.995kg.*

With increasing droughts and heavy rainfall, the soil needs to absorb and retain moisture – so mulch regularly and up to 100mm deep. Mulch with garden compost, green-waste compost (although this has a high pH) and any organic matter. Don't use peat. *Nick Coslett*

Years ago, my instructor at the New York Botanical Garden advised us to add triple superphosphate to the soil when planting new plants. Mix it in well, he emphasized, because it doesn't move in the soil but will stimulate root development when the roots come in contact with it. Spreading it on top does little. I have followed his advice with great success, especially when planting hydrangeas and roses. There are organic versions, fortunately.
Gwendolyn van Paasschen, Denmans Garden

Clay Soil

All is not lost with clay soil; it is great for water retention and nutritious for plants. It can be tough to work with. In my heavy clay garden, I have incorporated lots of organic matter to improve the soil. I have also added lots of grit. Beth Chatto advised in one of her books to use a wheelbarrow load per square metre. It's a lot of grit but has worked wonders in my garden. *Nicki Conlon*

Improve heavy clay soil with plenty of mulch autumn and spring *Lorna Luckhurst*

…And let the worms do the hard work! *Michelle*

Try using 'Strulch' as a mulch on your beds. (It's a light mulch made from wheat straw). It lasts about 2 years then fork in and re-lay. Very good at retaining moisture and the snails and slugs are kept at bay. *John Mankelow*

Mulch your borders and planters with compost or soil conditioner every year. Your plants will thank you for it throughout the year. *Paul Herrington, Grow Places.*

Dump your morning coffee grounds in your vegetable and flower gardens. *@ozaukeetalent*

The single most important thing in the garden is the soil. Soil is alive, it needs water and food just like us. *Stephen Mason, Community Gardener*

Always prepare soil well. Dig over with a spade in the autumn and add organic matter. Fork over in March, add well-rotted farmyard manure, then plant. *Susan Young, Susan Young Garden Design*

If you can't access, or don't want to use bought potting compost try using molehill soil. It is a fantastic weed-free, well aerated, well-structured loam. *Imogen Jackson, Head Gardener and horticultural therapist at Horatio's Garden, Midlands.*

Tree Mulching
Mulching offers an accessible and cost-effective means of improving plant and soil health.

- Assists in the regulation of both soil moisture and temperature
- Can act as a weed suppressant
- Can help minimize soil compaction
- Reduces run-off after heavy rains
- Adds organic matter to the soil
- Improves soil structure, nutrient value and water holding capacity
  Mulch is best composed of organic materials such as non-diseased leaf litter, seasoned tree mulch/wood chips, straw or hay as these materials will degrade over time.
- Apply mulches over damp soils during cooler months
- Spread to a thickness of 75-100mm (approx.)
- Keep mulches clear of direct contact with trunks/stems to avoid potential bark decay. *Nick Arnold, Consulting Arborist, Australia*

THE DARK ART OF COMPOST-MAKING

A compost heap… can be a tiny enclosed thing, but it is incredibly satisfying to see those peelings and dead leaves become a rich fibrous soil. *Dame Helen Mirren*

Learn how to make great compost. Start a worm factory. Get a Bokashi bin. *Isabella Tree, Knepp Rewilding Project*

The roots of tricky perennials such as ground elder and bindweed can be safely composted once they have completely dried out in the sun for a few days. *Helen Yemm, Daily Telegraph Columnist and author of 'Gardening in Pyjamas'*

I recommend 'Hotbin'… the size of a council refuse bin, you don't have to turn your compost, they're rodent-free and quickly recycle your leftovers and garden waste into fabulous garden compost. *Francine Raymond, Garden Writer*

I have a 'Hotbin' and love it. It took a while to get the ratio of green to brown right, but now we have copious amounts of lovely crumbly compost in weeks rather than months. Being smaller than a compost bay, and being self-contained it can easily fit into most gardens. *Mark Lane, Broadcaster, Writer, Garden Designer*

How to go about actually making the good stuff yourself

Composting *in place* is a tried and true way to utilize your kitchen scraps including eggshells and coffee grounds without having to manage a compost bin or heap. Simply dig a nice hole or trench, deposit your scraps and cover with soil. It's a great habit to get into. *Charlotte Blome*

Make your own leaf mould! Stick your collected leaves in black bags with a splash of water and leave for a year. We really should be avoiding the use of peat and leaf mould is a great alternative, the plants and planet will thank you... *Tom Cutter, Senior Gardener, Gledurgan Garden*

...The leaves will rot down over the year and you'll be left with a bag of wonderful leaf-mould to condition your soil. *Francine Raymond, Garden Writer*

...Leaf mould is black gold in the garden. At the time raking large amounts of leaves up is tedious but it's worth it. *Lee Dexter*

To make good compost using bins:
- Ensure the site gets plenty of sunshine summer and winter.
- External heat is essential to aid the rotting process, or you will have a slimy mess.
- Stand bin on blocks with a ground layer of bare branches.
- Shape a point on a broomstick's end to drill air holes through the material to ground level; keep them open. *Sue Bateman*

If you stand your compost-bin on chicken wire or similar the rodents shouldn't be able to dig their way in! *Anne Hawkins*

Save that old bit of carpet to keep the compost heap nice and warm as it ferments and provides the energy for the garden for the next year. *John Moore-Bick*

For those with a little kitchen compost container by the kitchen sink – put half a cardboard egg box container, or cardboard avocado/strawberry/raspberry tray in the bottom to soak up any moisture. It will compost down well when you chuck it on the main heap! *Penny*

Improve the appearance of the compost heap by planting *Symphytum grandiflorum* Hidcote Blue beside it. *Julia Sebline*

Consider creating a worm farm:
I recycle my kitchen scraps to my worm farm. Once the worms have done their job and created worm casting I mix it with my compost that is made from my three compost bins. The material that I compost comes from the garden pruning, hedge clippings and grass clipping and fallen leaf litter from my garden.

Mixing the compost and worm castings together creates my own potting mix, which I use to pot up various plants such as orchids, succulents and ferns. I also use the garden mix in some planting pots or as up top-up medium for my planter boxes.
Wayne De Klijn. Landscape Architect, Australia

WEED CONTROL

Pull up THAT weed because one year's leaving is 7 years' weeding.
Keith Matthews

Newspaper acts as an effective weed-proof mulch. Simply lay it
about four sheets thick over the weeds and cover with compost.
It will last for a year, when it can be reapplied if needed. Otherwise
it will rot and disappear, unlike some other inorganic mulches such
as weed control fabric. *Barty Meredith-Hardy, Professional Gardener*

Weedy veg patch? When the growing season is over cover the weedy
area with flattened out cardboard boxes (which you have saved!)
then weigh them down with compost from your heap and let the
worms, winter and nature do their work! Weed-free spring!
David Briggs,

Hastily pulled-up flowering willowherb, groundsel and other
weedlings with volatile seeds (and of course decapitated heads of
dandelions), should be dumped in a bucket of water to stop their
seeds from ripening and blowing about. *Helen Yemm*

One is based on a mediaeval idea. Boiling water on weeds. I use any
surplus water on weeds in paths and block paving. There is always
something left over after making a cuppa. The smaller the weeds the
better. Much better than using chemicals. I have been doing this for
30 years or more. *Michael Brown Garden Historian and Horticulturalist*

I have found that for long term weed control a good layer of some
organic mulch, such as compost, wood chips, leaf mould or straw
etc. works better than an inorganic weed barrier. The mulch slowly
breaks down and feeds the soil, and the few weeds that do grow in it
are easily pulled out by hand. Soil will not improve under a fabric,
and eventually the weeds do grow through it and then are very
difficult to remove. *Darius Winter*

Never let bindweed see a Sunday. Weed it out at least once a week
to weaken and eventually kill it. *Rozanne Delamore*

Hoe weeds when the ground is dry, as this will keep them under
control more efficiently than if you hoe when the soil is wet.
Sue Stirling

My best tips are: weed early on in the year, check garden for slugs and snails and move to your green waste bin as soon as possible – they'll be just as happy there. *Martha Krempel, Martha Krempel Garden Design*

'Weeds' are native wildflowers by another name and most are quite lovely and vital for British wildlife. *Isabella Tree, Knepp Rewilding Project*

NOTES & OBSERVATIONS

4. WATERING & FEEDING

WATERING

Water small seedlings from below. This relies on capillary action and helps to grow strong roots. *Mark Lane, Broadcaster, Writer, Garden Designer*

Water larger seedlings from above using a mister spray bottle. This way you are less likely to knock over the fragile seedlings. Don't forget to use a cover or humidity dome until the early germinating process is done to keep the moisture in. *Mark Lane*

Water your plants under cover in the early morning to conserve moisture loss and help to avoid powdery mildew and other fungal diseases. *Graham Smith*

It is always best to water young seedlings and cuttings with tap water to prevent rotting off. Collected rainwater is perfect for everything else. *Simon Newman. Professional Gardener*

When planting in late spring/early summer, make a little moat around the drip line of your plant. Scrape it out with your hand. This will help to retain moisture (watering or rain) in the area where the plant needs it most. The 'doughnut' will disappear during the season having given your plant a nice start in life. This might even help you to reduce your watering and makes sure you get the water where you need it most. *Fran Clifton, Head Gardener, Sir Harold Hillier Gardens*

Easier watering

Weave a seeping hose along rows of raspberries and strawberries, among crops, or alongside hedges and through flower borders. When weather is dry just plug on the main hose, turn on the tap, and water gently. It can even be attached to a water butt that recycles rainwater. Using a tap timer will automate the job by turning water on and off at the chosen time and duration, perfect if you're working away or on holiday. And it's so much easier than lugging a heavy watering can around! *Adam Pasco, Former Editor of BBC Gardeners'World Magazine*

Watering with a hosepipe:
One of the biggest problems gardeners find with hosepipes is gauging how much water the hosepipe is delivering to their plants. To improve this, fill a watering can up with water from the hose pipe and count how many seconds it takes to fill to the top. If the watering can is full after 60 seconds, the gardener will now know that after every 60 seconds they are giving one watering can worth of water to their plants. So simple, but, so useful. *Lisbet Rausing, Nicky Browne, Head Gardener, Wadhurst Park & Sara Jackson, Gardener, Rolf's Farm*

Watering pots:
It is often hard to judge how much water you are giving. Water your pot plants normally and leave to stand. After a while return and tip out a pot to see how much, if any, dry soil remains. It can be very informative. *Lisbet Rausing, Nicky Browne & Sara Jackson,*

Watering pots:
…is best done early morning or evening as watering in the midday sun can cause scorching of plants. Ensure the water is directed on to the soil when watering your plants as watering directly on the leaves or flowers will cause damage. *Linda & Marian, Cranbrook in Bloom*

Place water-absorbing gel, or products containing it in the bottom of pots which greatly reduces the need for watering. *@hazellawes*

Place gravel filled saucers under pots to cut down on watering but remember to remove them in late autumn to prevent roots sitting in water overwinter and pots being damaged by frost. *Stephanie Donaldson*

Better to thoroughly soak garden tubs every few days than give them a splash of water every day. *Nicky Robinson*

Prepare for rain!

In summer, when you finish watering the garden fill all your watering cans and leave them dotted round the garden so that you can easily do emergency watering of flagging plants. *Stephanie Donaldson*

Never leave an empty watering can! *Jenifer Morley*

After a dry spell… put out all receptacles to catch the rain. *Pat Keogh*

In summer months if something needs watering then water it, relying on forecasts of rain at this time of year is rarely enough. *Simon Newman, Professional Gardener*

Empty watering cans and turn them upside down at the beginning of winter so that they don't get damaged by frost. *Stephanie Donaldson*

Use sharp scissors to cut round the top of a 4-pint plastic milk carton to make a handy water carrier to keep by your water butt, for when you notice a plant in distress. *Gill Mullin*

Water plants well before applying a mulch. In hot, dry weather, water plants thoroughly in the evening. *Sue Stirling*

Collect as much rainwater as you can in water butts by attaching lengths of guttering to your shed, greenhouse, conservatory or other garden buildings. Rainwater diverters can also be installed in the downpipes from the gutters on your house. If you want to save more water, and have the space, join two or more water butts together with pipes so the butts fill in turn when it rains. *Adam Pasco, Former Editor of BBC Gardeners' World Magazine*

A few pieces of charcoal in the bottom of a water butt will keep the water sweet. *Stephanie Donaldson*

To ensure my houseplants are happy and healthy I only water them with rainwater. If you don't have rainwater, filtered water or boiled water cooled down will work too. If you use tap water, the chemicals in it can build up overtime. Not great for happy houseplants. *Nicki Conlon*

Studies have shown that watering newly-planted shrubs and trees less often but deeply, significantly promotes root development. I have followed this practice even more religiously here in Sussex where the soil is very well draining, making sure to water a larger area than just the immediate root ball.
Gwendolyn van Paasschen, Denmans Garden

Many perennials will do well without artificial watering and without feeding. The results, over time will be stronger and slightly lower growing which seldom require staking. In winter their natural architectural structure is revealed without artificial stakes or canes and with less impact on the environment. *Michael Walker, National Gardens Specialist*

Water your plants as soon as possible after planting. Sometimes a newly planted plant will wilt despite the soil being wet. This is termed "transplant shock" and it is a temporary condition. The plant is adapting to new growing conditions and possibly fewer roots. In order for the plant to cope it reduces foliage and flowers to match the remaining root system. Watering the first 2-3 weeks is most critical for actively growing plants, after which the new roots should be growing into the surrounding soil. *Anita & Tony Avent, Raleigh, USA*

Many garden vegetables and some bedding plants are best watered near the soil, keeping moisture off leaves, stems, and blossoms where it may encourage fungus and other diseases as well as attract insects. *Stacey Pagluica, Forever Gardens Inc, USA*

To facilitate better watering when planting trees, shrubs or even perennials, I dig the hole a little deeper than necessary and drop a few pebbles in the bottom. Then poke a tube onto the pebbles – best sloping out of the ground to at least a foot high (I use old drain pipe) Then you can pour water down the pipe instead of on to the surface. Less is lost to evaporation, and it encourages the roots to grow downwards. *Joy Virden*

If your plants in pots are struggling, even though you have watered them, it's likely that the compost is no longer absorbing moisture. Water just drains straight through and people may think that they have plenty of water, quite the opposite. To get water to 'stick' to the compost again add a few drops of washing up liquid for a week or two to the water and that should help! *Jane Buxton*

Stand humidity-loving houseplants, like orchids and *Calatheas*, on saucers of pebbles. When you water, the run-off will collect in the saucer. Then it will slowly evaporate, creating a humid micro-climate around your plant. Perfect! It's a great way to re-use water too. *Dr. Fay Edwards*

FEEDING

Natural Plant Feeds

Nettles are not your enemy. Collect them, put them in a bucket and fill with water. Leave for as long as you like until you feel that your vegetable patch needs an extra boost. Packed with chlorophyll and nitrogen. *Amanda Garratt*

Nettle plant feed (very smelly)
You need bucket or tub with lid, fill 3/4 full with water (preferably rainwater) cut nettles, loosely chop, insert into tub, put lid on, stir weekly, ready in a month. Dilute one-part feed to ten parts water *Michele Gamon*

…You will find it a richly nutritious feed for your tomatoes. Simply add to a watering can of water. *Malcolm Wynne*

Comfrey or nettle liquid plant food

Forget offensive-smelling buckets. Make small quantities of a potent brew throughout the summer by cramming a good handful or so of leaves in a recycled plastic bottle, topping it with water. Turned and shaken often, it takes two or three weeks or so to 'mature'. To use, dilute it so that it looks 'tea'-strength. *Helen Yemm, Daily Telegraph Columnist & Author of 'Gardening in Pyjamas'*

Creating your own home made, high potash liquid fertilizer from comfrey leaves is becoming quite popular but doing it in a bucket of water can be a rather long, smelly process! To make a quick feed just over half fill a blender with chopped comfrey leaves, then fill it to the top with water. Blend thoroughly and dilute the resulting liquid at the rate of 1 tablespoon per gallon of water. (The best variety of comfrey to use is Bocking 14 as it is a rapid grower and does not flower, so no problems with unwanted seedlings around the garden). *Diana Walton Head of Shows at RHS Malvern Spring Festival, Malvern Autumn Show.*

Make your own tomato feed by throwing the tomato side shoots into a bucket. Mix with water and leave to 'stew' for a few days. You know when it's ready by the smell. Pour into a watering can and have a nose peg at the ready when watering takes place. *Carlyn Kilpatrick, Horticultural Therapist, The Nurture Project*

Blooming Green Flowers offer their favourite recipes for peat-free compost:

Seed compost recipe
1 Coir bale, 15 litres water, 10 scoops fine vermiculite
five scoops sieved bark
1. Soak the bale in water in a plasterers' bath for 3 hrs.
2. Use a border fork to crumble it up. Add more water using a rose if necessary
3. Add the vermiculite and bark and mix well.
4. Transfer the finished compost to the tub trug and label.

Potting Compost Recipe
1 Coir bale, 15 litres water, 15 scoops medium vermiculite,
five scoops sieved bark, 420g Vegro coir nutrient pellets or 420g
coir nutrient base (smells!!)*
1. Soak the bale in water in the plasterers' bath for 3 hrs.
2. Use a border fork to crumble it up. Add more water using a rose if necessary
3. Add the vermiculite and bark and mix well.
4. Weigh out the nutrient and add
5. Mix well
6. Transfer the finished compost to tub trug and label.

*When using Coir nutrient base, transfer the mixed compost to plastic compost sacks and leave for at least one week before use.

Organic matter is the magic ingredient, it gives so many benefits to the soil which helps the plant grow. Best applied in the Autumn however anytime of the year will do. Use compost from a weed free source. Apply at least 5cm thick. Keep away from stem of plant. *Barty Meredith-Hardy, Professional Gardener*

A really simple tip is to feed your soil after the first summer show of flowers has finished. I just throw handfuls of granular fertiliser bought from any local nursery over the flower beds. I water it immediately and watch the plants perk up for a second late show of colour. *Roland Comet*

To increase flowering of annuals in patio pots or containers use tomato feed when watering at the usual dilution every other week. *Chris Walker*

I pulverize all my egg shells to powder and save them to mix in the soil of the growing bed I will be raising tomatoes in. I usually mix them in one week prior to planting. This little recycling trick will keep blossom end rot away from my tomatoes during their growing season. *Ilena Gilbert-Mays, North Carolina, US*

For roses use Epsom Salts
Mix 2 Tablespoons of Epsom Salts with 8 litres of water
Water around the stem of your roses once a month during March, April and May to get good healthy roses. *Arundel Castle Garden Team, also Jenifer Morley*

For roses, use Uncle Tom's Rose Tonic sprayed on the soil around plants from early bud formation until autumn. Spray at about 2 weekly intervals and you can combine a fungicide with the tonic as necessary. Details of how to buy the tonic are available on Google. *Chris Walker*

I use a natural organic fertiliser for the garden, as it is so important to put back into the soil what has been taken out by a year of growing, thereby continuing the natural cycle of everyone's daily enjoyment. *Valerie Singleton OBE*

5. PLANTING PERFECTION

Before you choose plants

Try to raise plants native to the area… they grow bigger and faster. *@queen_sticky*

Put the right plant in the right place – if it likes shade, give it shade; if it prefers sun, give it bright light. *Alan Titchmarsh*

Use the RHS website to check the plant you're planning to use will thrive – don't be tempted to buy random plants and plonk them in! *Jane Scott Moncrieff, Garden Designer*

Wait to see what is growing on its own, before weeding. Plants grow best when they have chosen where they want to grow. *Michelle*

Verbena bonariensis is my favourite plant but sadly makes a poor showing in our borders. However it self-propagates to the gravel in the garden paths and flourishes brilliantly. So trust your plants to know their best location! *Val Payne, Honorary Fellow of the RHS*

If you are a new arrival in a neighbourhood, always look to see which plants grow particularly well. This will save struggling to grow plants that may not like your climate or your soul *Edward Close-Smith (and also from Diana Walton)*

Try and live through each of the seasons before moving large shrubs or plants that you think you don't like. They might be there for a reason! *@Generous Gardener*

Many 'rare' plants are rare because they are difficult to grow and maintain in your soil (as I know). *Lady Sandwich*

Remember that like buying a house, 'location, location, location'. Really check out the position for the sun, wind and soil type of where you want to plant something. Does your plant like those elements? Having said that, plants like people, constantly surprise you with anomalies! *Dame Helen Mirren*

Plant research is the name of the game...
Jilayne Rickards, Jilayne Rickards Contemporary Garden Design

And... if you don't know how to look after it then you shouldn't buy it. *Tina Sales, Garden Designer*

Always buy healthy stock from a reputable supplier to prevent the spread of plant diseases – it's more important than you think. *Alan Titchmarsh*

Check how big a plant will grow (and also if it will spread too rapidly). It needs to have room to mature. If you cannot accommodate its ultimate size, find something else that will fit your space. *Alan Titchmarsh*

With global warming and warmer temperatures select plants accordingly. Choose hardy plants that can withstand drought otherwise you'll spend all summer watering and there will be hosepipe bans in the future! *Georgina Stewart*

When choosing plants in nurseries, don't necessarily go for the biggest or the ones with most flowers on. Instead select those with lots of new growth at the base, or plenty of developing buds.
Helen Yemm, Daily Telegraph Columnist & Author of 'Gardening in Pyjamas'

Things to remember when planting:

The bigger the pot, the bigger the hole you have to dig. So buy a plant in a smaller pot, dig a smaller hole (and wait for the plant to grow) and spend the money saved on another small plant.
@archiewonderdog

Spend as much on the hole as you did on the plant (well not exactly but you get my drift.) Good soil makes for good plants.
Alan Titchmarsh

When planting new plants make sure the roots have good contact with the soil. *Deborah & Michael Bedford*

Mycorrhiza applied to the roots of a plant (not sprinkled in the hole) will greatly assist it to establish.
Barty Meredith-Hardy, Professional Gardener

To avoid creating air pockets around roots when potting-on a plant into a larger-sized container, it is easier to run dry (rather than damp) compost down the sides as you fill it. Water thoroughly just once, then let the roots settle for several days before watering again.
Helen Yemm

When planting on a steep slope, as I have to do, it's easier – and safer – to use a hand mattock instead of a spade. Make sure you have a firm place for you and the plant to stand, use the mattock to dig the hole, trowel out the surplus soil and stockpile it above the hole. Once the plant is in the hole the soil can be drawn down and firmed around the root-ball. *Maurice Wilkins*

When planting trees and shrubs if the soil is dry, dig the hole and fill it with water and let it soak into the soil. If necessary do this two or three times. Ensure that the plant roots or root ball are moist then plant and mulch. Consider putting a perforated drain pipe down to root level to get future waterings to the right place.
Ken Turner

When planting a pot grown plant in the garden, only back fill the hole halfway, before firming the soil very well. Then fill the remaining hole with water until it is a puddle and does not drain away quickly. When the water has drained away, finished filling the hole but firm the soil very gently with your fingers. The plant will root down into the permanently damp soil and not in the dry surface soil. *Timothy Walker*

When planting, immerse the roots of the new plant in water for at least an hour. Dig a hole at least twice as deep as the plant root ball. Add some compost and dig it into the bottom of the hole. Fill the hole with water and let it drain away. Then refill with water again and let it drain. Put in the new plant, add compost and firm it down. Sprinkle on more water. then no need to water again, since the roots will go down to get the water. Watering later will only encourage the roots up to the surface where they will dry out.
Lesley Smith

If you want to move a plant at any time of year even when it is well grown and in full flower, dig a reasonably large hole and fill it with boiling water maybe up to three times before putting in your leaf mould or compost. This takes the chill out of the ground and the plant or shrub should settle nicely. *Julia Sebline*

Always plant your plant slightly higher in the ground than it was in the pot. Never deeper. Firm the ground around the plant and water in. As the freshly dug hole settles, the plant will also settle to the same planting level it was originally in the pot.
Robert Brett, Curator, RHS Garden Hyde Hall

When potting up a plant it's often easier to use the pot on its own as a sort of template, sitting it on a layer of compost inside the new pot and filling the gap between them with more compost, giving it a shake down. All you then have to do is to carefully remove the smaller pot and lower the plant gently into the hole. Tap it on the bench and it's sorted! *Maurice Wilkins*

Poor plant or poor growing plants? Don't just look at the top, look at the bottom and see what the roots are doing. The problem can often be found below ground level. *Robert Brett*

When planting or digging into hard soil move the trowel or spade from side to side keeping pressure on, it is far more effective than brute force alone. *Simon Newman*

Planting is best done in the spring or autumn, avoid the drying summer weather. But should you come to plant in the summer, fill the planting hole with water, then backfill as it drains through, helping to avoid the risk of your new plant drying out. *Tom Cutter, Senior Gardener at Glendurgan Garden*

Never be worried about moving a plant which is growing in the wrong place, or getting too big; I have had great success in moving all sorts of established shrubs – just make sure you water them well once moved. *Angela Monro*

Do not fear experimenting with plants, its half the fun and there is a great truth in the advice that "a plant should be moved three times before it finds its place" *Sarah Eberle, Landscape Designer*

Growing Ferns

Shady places suit ferns such as *Dryopteris erythrosora* and *Polystichum setiferum, Plumoso-Divisilobum* as well as snowdrops and *Cyclamen hederifolium. Roy Lancaster*

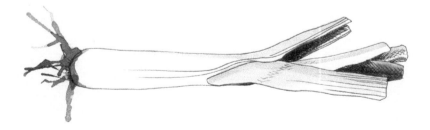

There are over 10,000 fern species and absolutely countless varieties and cultivars. They can be tiny, they can be huge, they can hug the ground, they can grow a trunk! *Maurice Wilkins*

There are ferns for every situation: dry, wet, full sun, shade or even aquatic situations. *Tom Cutter, Senior Gardener at Glendurgan Garden,*

It is great fun growing ferns from spores. I fill 3" round pots with compost, cut a piece of folded kitchen roll to fit over the surface of the compost and gently pour boiling water over the paper to sterilise the compost beneath. When it's cool, remove the paper, sow the spores on the compost and drop the pot into a transparent yoghurt tub, greasing and fitting the lid. Place in the shade and wait! *Maurice Wilkins*

Planting Trees

Tree Planting – when planting a new tree plant a length of pipe at the same time, laid vertically with one end in the planting hole and the other just above final soil level. When it comes to watering you can place a hose into the top of the pipe and water the tree right where it needs the water, i.e. at the roots. *Mark Lane, Broadcaster, Writer, Garden Designer*

When planting a tree always support it with a shorter stake rather than a tall one. A 30cm stake above ground will support a standard tree if a couple of strong tree ties are used with the proper cushion between stake and tree. This way the tree will be able to flex and grow its own 'muscle'. Ensure that the top tie is right at the top of the stake to avoid the tree rubbing the stake. *Maurice Wilkins*

Always make sure a tree's soil level in existing container is exposed and not covered in mulch which can rot the base and can cause infections in the tree. *Brandon George*

Often if you're unsure whether a newly planted tree or shrub is still alive someone will suggest scraping its bark to see if it's green. A sure way of letting disease into an already sick plant! An old gardener once told me to hold a branch of the sick plant tightly in one hand and a definitely dead branch of a similar size tightly in the other. The dead branch warms to your hand temperature quickly and if the other is alive and full of water it takes much longer to warm up! *Alan Mason*

If you have heavy clay soil and are planting a tree or large shrub, trying digging a square hole with corners. This will prevent roots from effectively spinning and not growing outside of the hole. It would also help prevent girdling roots as well. *Brandon George*

Growing Well

Many perennials will do well without artificial watering and without feeding. The results, over time will be stronger and slightly lower-growing which seldom require staking. In winter their natural architectural structure is revealed without artificial stakes or canes and with less impact on the environment.
Michael Walker, National Gardens Specialist

Don't be afraid to remove plants from flowerbeds to prevent overcrowding and competition for water, nutrients etc. Many spreading plants can tolerate being split and reduced in size to aid better growth. *Jenny Cowling*

Stakes & Support

For fun, try using sunflowers as supports for runner bean plants. Sow a sunflower seed into prepared ground or a suitable sized pot. Once the sunflower has achieved a reasonable height (30cms plus), plant the runner bean seed/plant beside the sunflower and train up the sunflower with the occasional use of twine where necessary. *Adam Piper*

Every year I plan to stake and support my tall herbaceous plants early in the season to allow them to grow through the supports. Peas or hazel shoots work well, along with metal frames or canes. I am always frustrated with the damage from the winds and rain if I haven't done this early enough. *Julie Comet*

Instead of always using bought canes for plant support I now keep my cut down raspberry canes and the thicker ones make good support and look natural and bend so you can tie them together at the tops. *Alison Beach*

Michaelmas daisies often grow so tall that when they are in flower they fall over if not staked, so at the end of June cut them back to 6-9 inches. They will flower slightly later but they will not need to be staked and they will not fall over. This works well for Aster divaricatus and Aster 'Little Carlow'. *Timothy Walker*

The best way I have found to support my plants are steel bow supports. Long lasting and easy to use, they hold up all sorts of perennials well. *Nicki Conlon*

NOTES & OBSERVATIONS

6. ROOTS, FRUITS & LEAVES

In mid-May a late frost murdered my runner beans. What a pitiful sight they were that morning, all flopped and flaccid. I mentioned this in my newspaper column and a churchgoer from Ledbury wrote with some old advice: beans should not be planted out until after Ascension Day 'and then they will rise safely towards Heaven'. This may not be the most scientific advice because the date of Ascension Day varies. I intend to follow it nonetheless. *Quentin Letts, The Times Parliamentary Sketch Writer*

I always knew you could grow plants between sweetcorn stems but it wasn't until the hot spring this year seemed to be cooking my spinach and beetroot seedlings that I thought I would give it a try. So I sowed a row of each vegetable between the already growing sweetcorn and they grew away happily. *Angela Baker*

When you are preparing veg, such as spring onions, lettuce or celery, do not throw away the ends as you can re-root these in water in a small tray on the windowsill. Then, once they have got some roots (a few weeks) plant them out in the garden, a pot or a raised bed. *Connor Smith, Horticulturist*

When growing leeks, I get small lengths of builders damp proof course (available from most builders' merchants) and wrap them around the leeks as a collar. This greatly lengthens the white edible barrel of the leek as the plant grows to maturity. Do however check that the collar does not become too tight as the leek grows. *Duncan Rouse*

We inherited our asparagus bed, and we had home-grown crop from Easter until the end of June. It takes three years for an asparagus bed to establish but it's worth the wait! Don't cut the spears in the first season, only cut a few in the second season, after which you'll see the results in the third season. Once the season has finished it is important to let the asparagus grow out to long ferns. *Sophie Allport, www.sophieallport.com*

Sow some radish thinly, with or next to rows of slow germinating veg seeds. They grow very quickly, help you to see where the lines are and you also get to harvest the radishes. *Edwin Mole, Head of Horticulture, Bristol Zoological Society*

Grow New Zealand spinach instead of regular varieties. They like a warm sunny position. Will grow in greenhouse or in pots. A few plants will feed a family as it spreads quickly. *John Mankelow*

When growing young leafy vegetables and roots always cover with a barrier to prevent pigeons stripping them as soon as your back is turned. *Simon Newman, Professional Horticulturist*

Boxes of old-fashioned dried peas are perfect sown thickly into a small amount of damp compost. Popped on a sunny windowsill or outside, they will reward you with cut-and-come-again fresh delicious pea shoots to add to a salad or stir-fry. Full of goodness, trim them before the tendrils begin to twirl to ensure they are tender and tasty. *Simon Lycett, Celebrity Floral Designer*

Grow some kale plants in your greenhouse beds over winter.
John Mankelow

You can grow salad leaves and lettuce and strawberries between rows of bean sticks to save space. They all prefer some shade and like getting watered with the beans. *Angela Baker*

Companion plant some vegetables to avoid pest infestation.
i.e. carrots and onions planted together should resist carrot fly.
John Mankelow

Some vegetables are attractive to look at, so you can mix them with flowers and shrubs. Ruby chard comes in lots of colours. Shrubby herbs such as rosemary, thyme and winter savoury look good, taste good and attract insects. *Michael Brown, The Garden Historian*

Buy a living salad from the supermarket and break it up into seedling plants which can then be planted out and grown into mature salads.
John Mankelow

Lots of climbing vegetables can be grown up perimeter fences or walls, as can fruit bushes. *Julia Collard*

If you have an old rainwater butt, saw it in half, fill with good compost and use it to grow radishes, beetroot, and especially carrots as it will be high enough to avoid carrot fly. *John Moore-Bick*

How to start off carrots

It can be hard to germinate carrots (and parsnips) – they often don't grow if you just sow them in the ground, so I do this:

1. Put some paper kitchen towel in a dish
2. Soak it in water
3. Sprinkle the seed over it
4. Keep it in the house so you can make sure it doesn't dry out
5. After 4 days, make a shallow drill (groove) in the soil
6. Put more water into the dish and carefully pour the water and seeds out along the drill
7. Keep refilling the dish until all the seeds are evenly poured out into the drill
8. Cover with soil.

Brian Hackett

Potatoes

Don't bother trying to grow varieties that can easily be purchased from a super market. Concentrate on the more unusual varieties such as Pink Fir apple which are perfect for summer salads. We were introduced to potato bags this year. They can be bought online, come complete with seed potatoes and can be re-used year on year. No need for digging, just plant the potatoes in a layer of compost and as the plant sends out new shoots, cover and continue. When it comes to harvesting, only dig down one layer. The rest of the new potatoes will stay safe until required. *Amanda Garratt*

Potatoes
Seed potatoes can be sliced into 'chips' after they have been chitted and each chip planted individually. Make sure there is a new shoot on each chip. *John Mankelow*

Squashes
I like to grow lots of different squashes, my favourite and most reliable though is Crown Prince which stores well for 4 months during the winter. I grow them in a hot bed. Make a wooden slatted bed, about 80cm deep and roughly 125cm by 250cm (depending on available space). Fill with different layers of rotted compost, manure, cardboard and importantly, plenty of un-rotted compost (we use grass cuttings). The un-rotted compost generates the heat. Plant 6 or so germinated squash seedlings on top in late spring/early summer. Watch your beautiful squashes grow as they tumble over the sides. *Bridget Fraser*

Keep a diary each year on growing times, feeds used and locations of plants to rotate crops. *Kevin Fortey, 3 times Guinness World Record Holder and current record holder for the World's Heaviest beetroot weighing 23.995kg*

Rhubarb!
I love it! Hot, cold, and delicious with custard. But in order to get the best results for the following year don't be tempted to pull the last few stems. Let them rot back into the plant and then cover them with a rich mulch. You will be rewarded next season! My three rhubarb crowns have moved house with me three times! *Sheila Kefford*

Rhubarb really benefits from a good mulching of manure in the winter and doesn't like being forced every year. *Nicky Robinson*

To harvest your blackcurrants just prune off the whole branch with the fruit on it and this acts to prune the old growth and harvest the currants easily at the same time. You can then sit at a table and remove the currants at your leisure. *Nicola Macnee*

Raspberries can also be grown along fences or walls by tying in/on. Caution – allow a good width for their roots which grow out sideways underground. However, if this happens you can dig the new cane up and fill in gaps or give them away. *Julia Collard*

Tomatoes
Blossom end rot is likely to be due to calcium deficiency; a tea spoon of lime when planting is helpful. *Lesley Smith*

In a hot summer, it is best to retain all the leaves, or the fruit will get sunburn – that's where the fruit turns yellow and hardens. *Lesley Smith*

Be consistent when watering – water every evening. In warm weather, water evening and also in the morning. *Lesley Smith*

If you grow tomatoes, always keep a salt cellar close by so that you can taste them properly. *Graham Peters*

Growing tomatoes on the patio and in grow bags, they can fall over quite easily in the wind as they grow tall. The grow bag is too shallow to put a support cane so fill a spare plant pot with soil and place behind it. Insert a cane and tie in the tomato plant.
Amanda Maruca

To grow healthy high-yielding tomato plants you need to cut out the side shoots when they appear between the leaf and the stem. But did you know you can create new tomato plants from those side shoots? Use a sharp pair of scissors or secateurs to cut the side shoot close to the main stem, being very careful not to damage the main stem. Plant your new tomato plant into a pot large enough to support the root system (which will appear in a week or two), but when you transplant the new plant out make sure you plant them much deeper in the soil. Voila! Free tomato plants. My friend recently ended up with 36 from 5 original plants. *Peter Field, Lord Lieutenant, E. Sussex*

When transplanting the plants into their final home. Always plant them deeper than the current soil level on the root. This greatly encourages better root growth. *Graham Smith*

In a cold snap bring young tomato seedlings indoors as they do not grow on when night temperatures fall below 10°C.
Nicky Robinson

When tomato side shoots are about 4 inches long pinch out and plant into a pot of suitable compost. When rooted plant out individually. Allow to have two trusses and then pinch out. This will give you a bonus of a late crop. *Richard & Sandy Roff*

To raise your tomatoes and sun-loving plants to the sky use right-angle brackets to attach leftover planks to the top of wooden fences, thus creating a shelf for sun-drenched *Echinacea* or tomatoes etc… all around at head height !!! *Michael Thatcher*

Not everyone is lucky enough to have access to a greenhouse. Sow a variety of cherry tomatoes for an abundant crop. They don't require as much sunshine as larger varieties and therefore ripen far more quickly. They are deliciously sweet and if you plant a selection of colours your salad bowl will look heavenly and as an added bonus you don't end up with masses of green tomatoes which then need making into chutney. *Amanda Garratt*

Herbs

Basil on the Windowsill. Basil needs to be sown early spring in pots on windowsills. Be generous with your seeds to ensure a full pot of fresh herbs. Keep watered. If the summer is hot, the plants can be moved outside to give a fabulous Mediterranean flavour to outside dining plus it is a 'must add' addition to a tomato salad.
Amanda Garratt

The only tip I've discovered that works well is with a basil. It seems to be the only herb that truly responds to cutting off the stems that go to seed and then will grow like new – not like most other herbs and veg that just keep going on to seed. *Sally Kelly*

If you are growing herbs then it is best to grow them in alphabetical order to help with identification. Some people think this is onerous and struggle to find the time but it's easy really, it's next to the sage. *Charlie Kefford*

If you have mint plant in a pot (which is, after all, the best place for one as they can get very invasive) and it is looking a bit woody in the centre simply take it out of the pot and split it down the middle with a spade. Then turn the two halves back to back and re-plant with the woody bit against the outside of the pot. Infill with some new compost, water well and the plant will soon revive. *James Alexander-Sinclair*

Try growing garlic chives. These have a wonderful pretty white flower from June to August, and the leaves and flowers are edible, with a garlic flavour. They are very hardy perennials and you can keep on harvesting from March to October. Easy to care for, they can be grown indoors or out, and the flower heads can be used dried, in flower arrangements. *Imogen Jackson, Head Gardener & Horticultural therapist at Horatio's Garden*

Crops for Free

Leave some crops and herbs, like rocket and coriander, to flower and set seed. Their flowers attract beneficial insects like hoverflies to feed and breed, and their larvae eat pests like greenfly and blackly. Wait for seed heads to form and seeds to ripen, then collect to sow, store, or use in cooking. Growing your own seeds saves you money too! *Adam Pasco, Former Editor of BBC Gardeners' World Magazine*

Grow edibles in with your ornamental plants. You don't need a full-scale allotment to grow delicious fresh picked veggies. There is a beauty in some vegetable plants that makes them look attractive and striking when planted amongst flowers in your back garden, or in pots on a balcony. The red stems of chard are particularly beautiful as a foil for red-and purple-leaved dahlias. Shaggy-leaved kale plants also benefit from the companion planting technique. When planted amongst tall French marigolds such as Harlequin and the pretty clary sage, the kale benefits from the hoverfly larvae they attract which eat the aphids and whitefly. *Izzy McKinley, Senior Kitchen Gardener, Arundel Castle*

Try growing flowers to eat. Violas, calendula petals, blackcurrant sage and lavender all make pretty additions to cakes, ice cubes or salads. Mallow flowers have an interesting texture, chive flowers have a delicate onion/garlic taste, garlic chives grow as an umbel of small pretty white star shape flowers which taste of garlic and nasturtium flowers have a delicious slightly peppery taste. Male courgette flowers can be stuffed and fried, but are lovely raw in a salad, and *Hemerocallis* – day lillies (be very sure not to eat other lillies) have fabulous bright petals great in a salad, or you can fry the bud, serve it as a fritter or tempura. *Imogen Jackson*

Using Heritage Seeds:

Much of the heritage of our plants has been eradicated; however, there is now a view that heritage seeds need to be used, as well as protected. Since the industrialisation of farming methods our heritage of plants seem to have largely disappeared. Heritage seeds come from open-pollinated plants that pass on similar characteristics and traits from the parent plant to the child plant. There is no concrete definition that every gardener uses to define heritage plants. Some people state that heritage plants are those that were introduced before 1951, while others state that heritage varieties are those introduced before the 1920s. In general, you should consider heritage to be seeds that are possible to re-grow and pass on from one generation to the next.

One important thing to note for heritage plants is whether they are organic or non-organic. In most cases, heritage plants are organic because they are generally only used by small-scale gardeners who do not use pesticide or other harmful chemicals. However, there may be minor cases when chemicals do get involved since heritage plants do not always have a similar level of innate protection that hybrid and GMO plants provide against diseases and pests.

Remember, heritage refers to the heritage of a plant, while organic refers to a growing practice. Heritage plants are generally known to produce better taste and flavour; their fruits/vegetables are also known to be more nutritious. They will take a bit more care than their counterparts, but in the long term it will be worth it!

Most importantly you would also be playing a part in preserving the genetic diversity of plants, for future generations to enjoy.
East London Garden Society

7. PETALS & POTS

What I love is a slightly wild feeling, with things like tomatoes, beans and cucumbers growing amongst the flowers. My two favourites at the moment are **Japanese anemones** and **cosmos**. They are so beautiful, and if you dead-head them regularly seem to go on and on. **Nasturtiums** give me great joy, as their leaves and flowers brighten every salad. I live, and garden, in hope!
Joanna Lumley OBE FRGS

What to plant?

American Holly (*Ilex opaca*) I have been growing it from seed for 40 years. It's a very unique plant adaptable in many zones as people think it's a tree or a shrub. *Matt Long*

To make **agapanthus** flower, they need to be crammed in together, ideally in a pot with no space between them. *Joy Moore*

Peruvian Lily (*Alstroemeria*) are beautiful and fairly easy to grow. After the first year don't deadhead but pull up the whole stem from the root. This encourages further flowering. *Annie*

Bougainvillea plants benefit from a spell outdoors in the English summer. I have found that the flower colours become more intense with more light and that aphids can be dispatched much more easily. *Nicky Robinson*

Be very careful where you plant the common **day lily** (*Hemerocallis fulva*) in your garden as they are very invasive and difficult to remove because of their tuberous roots. They will choke out other plants as they spread. *Tricia Palmer*

Camellias flower in the early spring, but the buds form in the previous summer. Best to water well in July and August and add an acid fertiliser. *Lesley Smith*

Some plants such as **cosmos** and **dahlias** can have the tops pinched out of them when about 6-8 inches high. This will make them branch and produce a lot more flowers on longer stems which are better for picking for the vase. *Rozanne Delamore*

For September and October flowering: **autumn crocuses, cyclamen, salvias, hesperantha**, and the **rose 'Iceberg'** which flowers till Christmas. *Lady Sandwich*

From a wheelchair or kneeling stool, a **cyclamen** corm is easy to plant. No digging a deep hole, just a shallow scratch. It will then produce long-lasting pink or white flowers, followed by beautiful bi-coloured leaves, and will seed itself all around the garden in shady places under trees and bushes, where you least expect anything to grow. *Sally Dudgeon*

Growing **clematis**: Place a flat stone or slate at the bottom of its stem to shade the roots. **Clematis** likes to have its flowers in the sun and roots in the shade! *Arundel Castle Garden Team*

Dahlias don't need to be lifted! Each year I shove a load of straw on top, use an old plastic bag to make it watertight, put some hessian over to make it look less unsightly and tent pegs to stop it blowing away. It does the job nicely. I don't need to disturb the plants and each year they come back. Occasionally I might water if there has been no rain, just to make sure they don't get too dry and then in spring, take it all away and put mulch over the top. *Naomi Ferrett-Cohen, Garden Designer*

If you are naturally a tidy gardener, but have ended up, as I have, in a country garden, then plant **erigeron** somewhere and it'll settle in everywhere for a more relaxed look; I have discovered recently it also forms very nice neat mounds that look especially lovely along the edge of a raised bed. *Elisabeth Rambridge*

To grow a standard **fuchsia**: In October as the leaves are falling, find a hardy variety which is 2-3 feet tall and choose two or three stems which should be as straight as possible. Cut off as close to the ground as possible just below a leaf joint. Choose a deep flowerpot, fill with a suitable compost and push the stems in 5-6 inches below the surface. Remove any foliage ensuring you don't damage the growing tip. Place in a greenhouse for the winter and if it is not heated wrap in fleece. Keep compost damp but not wet. In March you should have new shoots. After two sets of leaves pinch out to promote a bushy head. Plant each stem in individual pots when growing well. *Richard & Sandy Roffs*

Space in the border? If in doubt, plant a **geranium**. *Gill Burn*

Godetia make a pretty annual edging plant (sow the seeds straight in the garden) and they self-seed freely for the next year. *Julia Collard*

Plant trouble-free **hellebores** and **epimedium** (also known as barrenwort) – both have elegant leaves and provide ground cover. *Lady Sandwich*

When planting **hostas**, always plant **pulmonaria** with them. This will give you almost 12 months of interest with the pulmonaria giving you foliage and flowers in the winter/very early spring. Then the hosta leaves will emerge over the pulmonaria for the summer and autumn months. *Gillian Polley, Polley Garden Design*

To split **hostas**, put the spade right through the middle of a clump, then pop each segment in a pot, and they will reward you with much new growth. *Joy Moore*

Hydrangeas benefit from a helping of sulphate of potash around the roots in spring and autumn. *Lesley Smith*

Hydrangea arborescens 'Annabelle' is a low-maintenance plant for a larger garden as they can get to 3m x 3m: they're very easy to prune as they flower on the new growth, and like dappled shade or full sun. A sheltered area in better for them as late frosts can damage buds. *Shane Murphy, Garden Designer, Lavender Landcapes*

Grey foliage plants like **lavender** and *Convolvulus cneorum* cope better with hot dry weather but only when they are well-established. *Ken Turner*

Growing **crepe myrtle** (*Lagerstroemia*): make sure the base
of the plant stays dry in winter. Put the plant in the warmest and
sunniest spot of your garden and protect from fierce winds. Prune
lightly after the hardest frost and never after the end of July. No
severe trimming is required in natural soil, just some yearly clipping
of the offshoots will do. Remember that it takes a very long time
to grow to maturity and protect young plants for at least the first
4 years during winter. Ideally plant them in spring. *Geert Devriese,
Horticulturis, National Lagerstroemia, Laurus collections, Belgium*

Magnolias will flower better if you plant with ericaceous compost,
feed, and do not let anything grow around the base. I place a circle
of old bricks about a foot from the trunk and top up with ericaceous
compost and feed in Spring. Reason: the roots near the surface are
responsible for the production of flowers and they do not like to
compete with weeds or anything else! *Beth Andrews-Dawson Garden
designer and horticultural blogger*

Penstemons are an amazingly easy and long flowering perennial.
You can easily propagate your favourite by layering: just bend down
a stem and peg it, or just put a stone on it and hey presto in no time
at all it will root and you will have another plant. *Beth Andrews-Dawson*

Herbaceous perennial **peonies** do not like to be planted too deep
but tree peonies are the opposite. Heap up the soil a little around
the base of the latter and it will encourage flowering and the
development of more stems. *Beth Andrews-Dawson*

Plant a few ***Persicaria amplexicaulis***. The UK's most under-rated
plants, their dense leaf growth denies light to weeds, they flower
from June until the first hard frost, making them stunning value for
money. *Paul Mc Bride, Sussex Prairie Garden*

Salvias: An easy way of multiplying your stock is to check for suckers as these propagate well and easily. If you dig up tender ones and keep them in a greenhouse over winter they are very readily divided in early summer the following year. *Annie*

Keep experimenting! We decided to create two lavender beds for the glorious scent and beautiful colour, but enjoyed it for only a couple of years before it started to slowly die.

It was a huge disappointment and I racked my brains for a replacement that would give a similar dense blue haze. One day while visiting Wellingham Herb Garden in East Sussex I spotted what I was looking for – it was **catmint**, (*Nepeta*) surrounding an antique sundial and it looked stunning. That was the moment I decided to replace the lavender. I bought established plants, spaced them sparingly and the following year I took cuttings.

To my delight they rooted and flourished. Now the beds looks glorious every year and the luminous blue flowers bloom most of the summer and I'm thrilled with the result. What's more you don't have to worry about accidentally cutting into the old wood as you do with lavender, just get in there with a hedge cutter and level it. I can highly recommend catmint for anyone who has struggled with lavender.

If you decide to go the catmint route I hope you have the same success. *Sandra Beck*

If yours is a small garden beware of planting perennials that spread quickly like **periwinkles** (*Vinca*), **Japanese anemones**, non-Chinese **epimediums** like *E. pinnatum, Acanthus mollis*, free seeding **geraniums** and most bamboos. Look to clumpers like **Aster x frikartii, hostas, lilliums, peonies** and **kniphofia**. *Roy Lancaster*

Bare spaces in sunny places sow with colourful annuals like **Californian poppy, cosmos, larkspur, love-in-a-mist**, *Echium vulgare and Orlaya grandiflora. Roy Lancaster*

Masses of fragrant **sweet peas:** they seed in well cultivated soil where you want them to grow and flower on the 10th October each year. Just protect from mice and slug attack and insert pea sticks for support in March to get masses of long-stemmed flowers from May to August. Choose fragrant Spencer types including HI Scent. *Peter Seabrook*

Start off Sweet Peas in the greenhouse in early autumn. Prune them back if they grow well and then they will flower early in the spring (April onwards). *John Mankelow*

Buy British flowers to reduce your carbon footprint and chemical use. Look at the Flowers from the Farm website for your local flower farmer. *Rozanne Delamore*

Roses

My real love is **roses**. I love bunching the pinks, reds and yellows together, they look quintessentially English and quite old fashioned but brighten up a neutral corner in a room. It's all about bringing the outside in. Cutting, pruning and dead heading roses is key to get the most from them and you always need a good pair of gardening gloves around roses. *Sophie Allport, sophieallport.com*

Roses are much easier than you think to grow from cuttings. Simply take a bit of this year's growth (about the thickness of a pencil) about 30cm long: cut above a bud at the top and below one at the bottom. Strip off all the leaves except the top ones and plant them (in part shade) in a trench (or a pot) with about ³/₄ of the cutting underground. Water well and leave alone for about a year. Sounds like a lot of faff but is very satisfying and saves money! *James Alexander-Sinclair*

Roses tend not to like being grown alongside other plants so keep some space round them. *Julia Collard*

Use mycorrhizal fungi (Root Grow) when planting roses, especially bare-rooted roses. Once the rose has been soaked for 8 hours before planting hold it over the hole and sprinkle mycorrihizal fungi over the roots so it sticks to them, the rest goes into the hole. Then plant it as this will give the rose a better chance of establishing quickly. *Arundel Castle Team*

Leave spent flowers of roses at the end of the season if the species bears ornamental hips. *Sally Cragg, Gardener at Madingley Hall, University of Cambridge*

To prevent blackspot on roses, treat the soil around the rose as well as the foliage. Blackspot is a fungus that lives in the soil and fungus likes damp so autumn/winter is an ideal time to lay dormant in the soil. When the sun arrives in the spring the spores SPRING into action and re-infect the plant. Also, keep soil around the rose free of dead leaves, debris etc as fungus loves this decomposing matter to live on. *Carol Smith, Garden Design Consultancy*

Encourage climbing and rambling roses to produce more flowers by tying the stems horizontally or wind them around supports. In the spring this reduces the sap flow to the upper most buds and encourages buds lower down the branches to burst into action, thereby ensuring a greater number of flowers and produced. *Steve Catchpole, Alder Gardening Services*

POTS

When growing plants of any size I remove the base of the pot and make sure the roots can go into some soil below (you may need to remove some slabs/concrete directly underneath). This way the pot can't be stolen, never blows over and after the first few months you will never have to water or feed again. The plant will look so much healthier than if it was left in a pot with a bottom. For more details see: My YouTube channel 'Baseless Pots the Ultimate Time Saver and Design Hack.' *Bunny Guinness, Bunny Guinness Landscape Design*

If you're wondering if a container display has enough texture, consider taking a black and white photo of the display. If a good display has enough texture you won't need colour to see it in the photo. *Brandon George*

Think outside the box, when growing flowers and salad crops and veggies, mix them up into pots and planters, the effect is a riot of colour, texture and fragrance. *Simon Lycett, Celebrity Floral Designer*

You can have whatever you like in pots - just follow the rule of thumb that if the plant doesn't do very well, take them out and don't plant them again. Hydrangeas will be fine as long as there's enough room for their roots, and that the pots are kept irrigated, out of blasting sunlight. The colour is due to acidity of soil - Google it. But essentially you need to make the soil more acid if you like blue: acid mulch is a way to do this if you can't be bothered to replace the soil completely. *Jo Thompson, Jo Thompson Landscape & Garden Design*

The key thing is to remember that whatever you plant in your pot, it won't survive on its own. By putting a plant in a container, it makes it totally dependent on you for water and food for survival. *Matthew Berridge, Zoo Gardener*

When planting in pots or tubs, I make sure the bottom layer is a mixture of crocks of all sizes, mixed with a little compost for drainage. *Lady Arabella Lennox-Boyd, Garden Designer*

Line terracotta pots with layers of wet newspapers before planting. *Julia Sebline*

Select the correct size of pot for your plant. Do not let plants become pot bound, however, some plants do not like being re potted into oversized pots. *Cranbrook in Bloom*

Some plants do not like direct sunlight so be aware, that some shade may be required. *Cranbrook in Bloom*

The garden needs to suit the climate so it will survive in the climate. Plant in the ground (rather than in a pot). Tragic to see so many people in Australia lose gardens they had built up over 50 years or more due to the drought. If I plant something new I will water it briefly, otherwise it has to survive.
To summarise my hints are:
1. Plant in the ground
2. Plant to suit your climate
3. Put down newspaper and mulch to inhibit weeds
   and maintain moisture
Trish Evans, Sydney, Australia

Feed container grown plants repeatedly through the growing season for best results. *Nicky Robinson*

Feed with seaweed extract as a liquid in the first half of the summer. When your young plants are past 6 leaves, dilute seaweed extract into a water sprayer and spray the plants early in the morning on a windless day. The plant absorbs the feed and when done little and often between May and July produces strong sturdy plants that are less prone to disease. *Chris Collins*

When re-potting a plant have the old pot as a template in the larger potand fill round the sides with compost. *Duncan Rouse*

Perfect Potting Soil Combo: Large bag (5.9 kg) potting soil, 2 cups general growing medium, 2 cups dry manure. Water and sunlight in moderation. An abundance of kind words and soft music. *Joan and Ted Berkey*

The compost you use needs to be the right compost for the job as established plants will need different compost from cuttings. Check the compost back for guidance. *Cranbrook in Bloom*

A handful of alpine grit on top of the compost helps to retain the moisture and make it decorative. *Cranbrook in Bloom*

One of my favourite plants for a container is Hakonechloa macra 'Aureola' with its golden grassy foliage, so dainty. Raise the container up and enjoy it at all the more. Its deciduous so nothing to show for the winter, but it certainly earns its place from late spring to autumn. Ideal for shade or semi-shade. *Kathy Brown*

For Summer Baskets: Use a large selection of different species to provide summer flowers from June to October. My suggestions for drought-tolerant (i.e. good if you are hand-watering!) plants: ***Bidens, Diascia, Felicia, Helichrysum, geranium*** (*Pelargonium*), ***Plectranthus, Scaevola and Verbena: Bacopa*** is a useful trailing edge and you could consider scaevola instead of **lobelia** as a trailing edge plant. **Heuchera** and trailing **Heucherella** provide various coloured foliage for background to flowers. ***Carex* 'Everillo'** is one of my favourite ornamental grasses that can be used in summer and autumn baskets and containers. *Terry Bane*

For autumn baskets include: – **Pansy**, *Polyanthus* and newer varieties of *Bellis, Carex* and varieties of **Ivy**, *Astelia* 'Red Devil' *Erysimum* 'Apricot Twist' and 'Spice Island', *Hebe* **'Purple Shamrock'**, *Libertia* **'Goldfinger'** and *Viburnum tinus.*
Terry Bane

Bulbs

Easy bulb planting. It is great to plant lots of bulbs for spring colour in autumn. A really quick and easy way to do this is to use a bulb auger attachment to a drill. They can be expensive, I have had great success using a flat wood drill bit and a wood extension drill bit at a more reasonable cost. Be careful where you are drilling and don't hit any stones. Protective glasses would be a good idea! *Nicki Conlon*

When you buy expensive bulbs like **lilies** pull off a few scales and dip them in fungicide. Put the scales into sandwich bags with some vermiculite. Store in dark at 20c. New bulbs will form on each scale after 12 weeks. Pot on and grow on to flowering size. This takes about 3 years. This is a cheap way of increasing your bulbs.
Quentin Stark, Hole Park

Bulb planting in Kent (i.e. in heavy clay): It's common sense if you think about it: look at the bulb and imagine it sitting in our Wealden clay for five months. Disaster. So if it's been raining for weeks, just be patient and wait a while. They won't come to any harm by going in a few weeks late, as long as they have been stored somewhere cool and dry. Bulb planters really take the hard work out of the job: and bulb planters with long handles are actually a stroke of genius – no bending down, no muddy knees and the bulbs get planted to the right depth. *Jo Thompson, Jo Thompson Landscape & Garden Design*

Plant **tulips** in late October/November at least 10cm deep. Plant them close together in your pots to give a big impact. Use different height tulips in pots to give structure. Mix your early-, mid- and late-flowering tulips to extend your flowering time and in borders plant in subtle swathes. *Arundel Castle Team*

Plant tulips in baskets made of wire netting with a bent hazel rim if you need to lift tulips after flowering. This ensures that none are left in the ground. *Julia Sebline*

For a wonderful display of spring bulbs why not make a lasagne? Partly fill a large plant pot with compost, plant tulip bulbs of your choice quite tightly and cover with a layer of compost. Then plant a layer of hyacinth bulbs, layering them with more compost. Plant a layer of crocus into this and top off with a final layer of compost. The succession of bulbs in spring is worth the effort, and the wait. *Anne F*

Always plant more bulbs than you think you need and always scatter them and plant exactly where they land. That way they pop up looking natural and not like a neat and tidy city park! *@Generous Gardener*

Remember that tulips do not need to be perfectly planted in your garden in straight lines or tight groups. Don't be scared to throw a handful of bulbs (any odd number will do but we find 5 works best) into your borders and plant them where they land. Your efforts will be rewarded in Springtime with fantastic, naturalistic bulb drifts – remember there is no such thing as a straight line in nature!
David Massey, David Massey Garden Design

On **Bluebells**: Make sure you buy the native ones which are labelled as *Hyacinthoides non-scripta*. These are the common ones which do have a sweet scent, not the Spanish bluebell which we need to avoid as it has a habit of swamping. And no scent. Double trouble. Throw a handful of the common type under trees and then plant them as deep as you can, at least 10cm and you'll have drifts of blue (and white – yes white are blue too) in your garden forever.
Jo Thompson, Jo Thompson Landscape & Garden Design

8. SNIPPING, SHEARING & SHAPING

Don't butcher your plants – check their pruning requirements and then cut judiciously. *Alan Titchmarsh*

Prune in a rage! *Sir Charles Fraser*

Get to grips with pruning your flowering shrubs – the harder, the better. Unpruned shrubs lose all their shape and flowers. *Sarah Wilson*

If you are intending to do any heavy pruning, please check very carefully for bird's nests. *Dave Risley, Folly Wildlife Rescue Trust*

When pruning or coppicing willow or hazel, always do it with a waning moon. *Lady Arabella Lennox-Boyd, Garden Designer*

Remember to 'Chelsea Chop'… a technique that you perform around the time of the Chelsea Flower show to check the growth of plants that are inclined to get leggy! It may seem counter intuitive to chop off about a third to half of the growth and even some flowers in May but it has several uses – it stops them getting leggy and falling onto lawns and getting mowed off so they look ugly; it stops more vigorous thug plants drowning those that have better manners; it promotes a shorter less unruly regrowth with more – possibly smaller flowers – and it prolongs the season of interest. It's not suitable for all plants but things that have growth habits like *nepeta, agastache*, some salvias and even the larger sedum really benefit from this treatment and you don't have to do them all – just the odd one or two plants in any clump around the garden so you extend that season of interest. *Gary Brown, Head Gardener at Private Estate*

A plant wants to grow, flower and set seed – that's its sole purpose - to continue its genetic line so if you stop the flowers on that plant going to seed (by dead heading) the chemical messages that the plant gets are that it hasn't set seed so it will try to flower again in order to make the seed! So by dead heading you get more flowers! *Gary Brown, Head Gardener at Private Estate*

It's well-known that serious dead-heading is important before a summer getaway, but I had always been timid until last year. I plucked up courage to strip every rose, helenium, dahlia, knautia, cosmos, tithonia, sweet pea and antirrhinum of its blooms, filling two buckets of flowers for a friend. The garden was entirely green when we left, but, on our return after three weeks in early September, it was a veritable feast of colour. *Vanessa Berridge*

When dead heading roses, do so as soon as petals begin to drop; don't pull them off, prune to the first outward facing 5 leaves. *Lorna Luckhurst*

When deadheading dahlias - remember the pointy heads are the spent flowers and the round heads are to come. *Sally Cragg, Gardener, Madingley Hall, University of Cambridge Institute for Continuing Education, also from Petra Venton*

Cut the dead heads of flowers at least twice a week to encourage more flower buds to appear. *Julia Collard*

Remember to give all your leafy herbs a good haircut in early May, to ensure they refresh and regrow through the summer. This works especially well for mint and chives. *Simon Lycett, Celebrity Floral Designer*

Cut back your *Alchemilla mollis* (also known as Ladies Mantle) hard before you go on your August summer holiday. If it is very dry give it a good soak too. You'll be rewarded with beautiful green growth on your return. *Petra Venton*

Pruning Wisteria

Prune first in early summer around about July – take back to 4 buds and then prune again in winter – January is best, take back to two buds and this will make flower buds for spring. *Andy Smith, Head gardener, Aspley House*

Wisteria not flowering? In late summer, cut the long wispy growth back to 5 buds, then the following February reduce these stems to 2 or 3 buds. And don't feed it. *Rupert Loftie.*

Prune your Wisteria in September or October to keep it neat. If you prune them in spring or summer it encourages the plant to send out too much growth. *Bronwen Glazzard*

Pruning Tips for Roses;

1. You shouldn't prune until late February.
   If you prune too early, our increasingly mild winters encourage premature bud growth which get damaged by later frosts and drying winds in April.
2. The pruning mantra is cut out dead, diseased and damaged wood. Do this before attempting to prune.
3. For Shrub roses (Old varieties and English Roses) to help focus on the shape you want invert your hand and fingers to produce a goblet shape – this is your template!
4. Clear the centre of the bush of any intersecting, inward-facing and rubbing branches.
5. Once the structure is clean and clear – prune back to an outward-facing bud.
6. Then feed – feed – feed.
7. For Climbers – cut out any wayward branches OR tie them in securely before the winter to avoid rubbing damage.
8. Use the Pruning Mantra as above!
9. Fan, basket-weave or espalier BUT always tie the branches securely to a wired wall or fence or post. Note; never tuck branches behind wires. This will avoid much aggravation when you come to prune or reshape in the future.
10. Prune back side branches to 2/3 buds.

Susan & Stephen Moir

When pruning shrub roses, try to create a 'goblet' shaped plant, with space in the middle to avoid 'crossing' branches, which can lead to damage. Prune with a slanting cut to help rain run off the freshly cut area of the branches. Always prune out weak, dead or damaged branches. If a rose bush has black spot, gather up fallen diseased leaves from the ground, and dispose of them, to avoid the spores spreading. Don't put them into your compost bin. *Sue Stirling*

Remember 'growth follows the knife' – any plants sole purpose is to flower and set seed to continue the line – if you take away the seed potential (spent flowers) the plant will do its best to flower again! *Gary Brown*

Pruning for shape – from a blob to tree

Get to know your subject, really look at the trunk and branches and decide on the contours you want. If you are nervous, start with the dead, damaged and diseased. Remove dead ends and oddly angled wayward branches but always follow the contours to check you're not lopping off something you want to keep and cut neatly near where it joins the branch or main stem. *Rhona Port*

Lifting the skirts (sounds rude but is an actual Old English gardening term). This is when you cut lower branches to thin out dead matter and raise the canopy. This is useful for underplanting as well as giving the impression of more space. Particularly good in hebes where lower branches often do die and can make a plant look messy and blob like. *Rhona Port*

Sculpt if you can't manipulate. A mature plant may not lend itself to being manipulated (for example topiary) or having its branches bent to shape. Generally this tip is for small trees or shrubs that tend to have thicker stems. Remember conifers, once cut, tend not to regenerate. *Rhona Port*

Check your progress as you work to see how the tree is looking so from a blob you can end up with a tree. *Rhona Port*

Pruning flowering shrubs at the right time of year will help to reduce time toiling in the garden and will give maximum flowering impact. *Philadelphus* ought to be pruned 4-5 weeks after it has finished flowering (usually around July). Young shoots for next year are already on the way. Prune out all flowered wood and any branches which are broken, dead or are congesting the shrub too much. Airflow is important for a healthy shrub. The shrub now has time to carry on producing flowering wood right up to the frost. It will not outgrow its natural size. No need to cut it a second time. *Forsythia* in May, spring-flowering *Spiraea* in May, summer-flowering *Spiraea* in winter. The shrub will usually tell you. *Franziska Clifton, Head Gardener Sir Harold Hillier Gardens*

Don't be afraid to prune plants hard, most will take it and respond well. If they don't you've created an opportunity for planting something different. *Nick Coslett*

The fresh young leaves of *Spiraea japonica* "Goldflame" are a soft golden yellow, those nearer the tips flushed with coral. If you are prepared to sacrifice the arguably undistinguished pink fluffy flowers by trimming 3 cms or so from the end of the shoots you'll be rewarded with a fresh flush of lovely new leaves. This can even be repeated a couple of times during the growing season. *Judith Strong*

On a larger scale *Cotinus coggygria* Grace with its glaucus mature leaves and bronzy aubergine new ones can be thought of as a shrub rather than the substantial tree it could become. By stooling it back to around 40cm in March you will forego the smoky flowers but produce long wands of extra-large leaves which look particularly stunning back-lit by the sun. As they become longer, leggier and greener the tallest third can be cut back by half. By repeating with the next third and so on it will continue to produce bronze leaves throughout the season and then succumb to winter in a blaze of crimson glory in late November. *Judith Strong*

Try cloud-pruning an evergreen myrtle, showing the stems and keeping lots of space between 'clouds' to create a lovely feature within 2 years. *Angela Goddard*

9. ESSENTIAL KIT

Essentials
- A Niwaki Hori Hori knife (absolutely indispensable)
- Felco secateurs (the ones with the swivelling handle makes it easier to cut bigger stems.
- Sneeboer small onion hoe (expensive but SO fabulous for weeding large areas relatively quickly)
- Mantis rotavator (ultimate girl-power machine)
- A leaf rake (forget the deafening leaf blower – you get a great workout with a rake and it's cheaper than going to a gym!)
- A border fork (large forks are too heavy for me for any length of time)
- A long-handled bulb planter (you'll hurt your wrist using the small ones unless you've got loose soil/less than 20 bulbs to plant!)
- Good edging sheers (hmm. Hard to find – mine are Wolf ones)
- And I'm never without Showa gardening gloves (Summer & Winter weight). *Fiona Wright, Professional gardener*

The best tool I have ever had for weeding is produced by a Japanese company called Niwaki and the tool is called Hori Hori – it is like a flat bladed wide knife. They also do lots of other tools which are all fantastically well made – I also love their Golden Spade.
Their catalogue is a delight. *Tricia Palmer*

My best garden gloves are Showa, I wear the green ones.
Lady Arabella Lennox-Boyd, Garden Designer

A builder's pointing trowel is the perfect tool for weeding amongst mat-forming and low-growing alpines. *Gill Mullin*

I find using small dead-heading snippers useful for dead-heading annuals such as petunias and geraniums. *Chris Walker*

A tripod ladder is essential if you have tall hedges. Safety First! *Susan Bowie*

Avoid using a ladder as much as possible by using long-handled tools. There is a range of tools available such as loppers and secateurs that are effective up to 3 metres. This makes a lot of high up jobs quicker and safer. *Barty Meredith-Hardy, Professional Gardener.*

If you use battery-powered tools e.g. lawn mower, hedge trimmers etc, always have two batteries – so that one is on charge at all times. *Susan Bowie*

A tool-belt equipped with your most used tools is very handy. A pair of secateurs, trowel, pruning saw, garden knife and sharpening stone can be popped inside: these will do for most incidental jobs around the garden and saves constantly walking back to the tool shed. *Barty Meredith-Hardy*

Keep cutting tools sharp. It makes the work easier and safer. *Michael Brown, Garden Historian & Horticulturalist*

I always have secateurs in my pocket when walking around the garden as there is always something lovely to pick for the house. *Lady Arabella Lennox-Boyd*

Every gardener needs two pairs of secateurs. One that can be slightly abused for 'rough' jobs, and one kept in pristine condition for 'posh pruning'. *Helen Yemm, 'Daily Telegraph Columnist, author of 'Gardening in Pyjamas'.*

A strip of brightly coloured tape around the handles of elegant (and expensive) wooden-handled tools helps to make them harder to mislay. *Helen Yemm*

Dark brown twine is more subtle than green or even 'natural' coloured versions. Aubergine-coloured (yes, there is such a thing) is even more so. *Helen Yemm*

If space is short or money tight a cold frame will do the job of a greenhouse. *Ellie Cochrane*

Secateurs that stick usually just need a good wash (to remove accumulated dried sap from the blade), followed by a dab of WD40 or tea tree oil. *Helen Yemm*

Choose tools which work for you! If you are slight, find a light fork, if you are stronger, choose something heavier... if a kitchen fork does the job... use that. Today, garden centres are awash with different-sized spades and forks. Felco secateurs have a good range for men and women. Kneelers keep yours knees dry and are great to help older gardeners rise from their beds! *Heather Fooks*

Recycle, re-use

Rather than purchasing the newest equipment check out second-hand tools and equipment online or at local market stalls or flea markets. These tools are inexpensive to purchase and tend to be worn-in and comfortable, like an old pair of slippers! Before buying them, you can pick them up, feel their weight and balance.

Interestingly, many older tools possess an elegant quality and design which makes them efficient and comfortable to use. It is also reassuring to know that a fellow gardener has used them, and that they have a history. *Dean Peckett, Head of Horticulture, Arne Maynard Garden Design*

We have three shops near us taking old British-made tools and making them feel like new. They are amazing quality and they look brilliant. Plastic does tend to be a point of weakness especially plastic handles on forks and spades… also, car boot sales or Freecycle are a great source for old pots. *David Ware, Edible Culture*

Use plastic-free rabbit guards and ties when planting trees. Guards made from recycled cardboard last exactly the correct time it takes for a tree to establish… and use jute netting and string instead of plastic netting and string. With a crop like beans, jute is brilliant because you can rip down the whole plant string and all at the end of the season and bung it on the compost heap. *David Ware*

Kit Maintenance

Wash or brush the soil off your metal tools after use. Use a handful of grass, a brush or oily rag. This will look after the metal, as will oiling them at least once a year. A cheap vegetable oil will do the job. It will keep them in good condition, sharper longer and far more enjoyable to use. *Lisbet Rausing, Nicky Browne, Head Gardener, Wadhurst Park & Sara Jackson, Gardener, Rolf's Farm*

At the end of a long season of gardening, treat your wooden handled tools to a good sanding with fine grit sandpaper and an application of boiled linseed oil. The smooth handles will be a joy to use next time. *Charlotte Blome*

Annually coat your trowel and fork handles with olive oil as most of the damage done to hand tool handles is by woodlice in storage areas. The little eaters of anything wooden won't touch olive oil and the handles have a much nicer glide throughout the planting season. *Dan Williams, Senior Head Gardener & Garden Lecturer*

Regularly sanding and treating your hoe shaft with olive oil reduces blisters and splinters on softwood handles. *Dan Williams*

When storing any metal tool always remove soil and moisture and give a quick wipe over with 3-1 oil, as just one winter can cause rusting and this makes the job much harder over time due to rust pitts holding onto soil and clay particles. *Dan Williams*

Specific tools for specific challenges

A padded garden kneeler/seat with handles is invaluable for most gardening jobs. It can also be used to help you get to your feet again. *Andrea Ballard*

A 2- or 4-wheel wheelbarrow or cart that can be pulled or pushed can be more useful than a one-wheel wheelbarrow. It should be more stable and easier to balance. It will also mean you won't have to make multiple journeys carrying garden rubbish and tools. *Andrea Ballard*

Build yourself a simple kit in something you can sit on. I can't dig or lift and I have found over the years that I can do most of my garden jobs from my work stool with a pair of good extendable secateurs, a small knife, a ball of string, a hand trowel and hand fork. Over the years I have built my garden to fit my disability, so that I no longer need to stretch, that means I can use lightweight hand hoes or soil cultivators from my stool. My problem is tidying up, I can't bend and I often lose my balance. So, a couple of years ago I had the idea of using litter picker grabbers, I can now easily pick up any leaves, stems or even spent flower heads from borders or veg beds and put them in a pop-up tidy bag. *Andrew Oldham*

If you have mature apple trees long handled fruit pickers make light work of an otherwise tricky job. You can make them at home with a pole and large fizzy pop bottle with the bottom part cut out! *Camilla Bassett-Smith, Horticultural TV Producer*

The most useful and practical advice that I ever received came from Lord Carrington, Margaret Thatcher's first foreign secretary who famously resigned over the invasion of the Falkland Islands and a politician I much admired while growing up.

On returning from the Second World War (and winning the MC) he and his young wife took over the running of the family estate in Buckinghamshire and set about creating a garden from scratch in the grounds of an eighteenth-century manor house they took on at Bledlow, the family seat having been too large to maintain. From what started as a working farmyard came one of the prettiest and most interesting domestic gardens of the post-war period. And Lord Carrington's advice? "Never go into the garden without a pair of secateurs."

And it is true, even if just nipping outside with a sneaky cup of tea and a paper you can guarantee to find a bramble, dead head, stubborn branch or athletic weed demanding attention. I keep several pairs, so there is always one by every door!
Rt Hon Lord Barker of Battle PC

10. PESTS & OTHER UNWANTED VISITORS

109

Wherever there are vegetables there will be bugs and pests. Embrace them. You may not get the best crop of brassicas but you will have a plot filled with beautiful butterflies. Alternatively, liberally scatter nasturtium seeds. Great for salads to add colour and the aphids love them. *Amanda Garratt*

Ask yourself if you need pesticides. *David Ware, Edible Culture*

To avoid using pesticides use the V-shape on your hose twice a week to spray upwards for a couple of minutes into a *Pieris* or any other shrub which is infested with lace bugs. Use this method also on box caterpillars. *Sue Rowles*

Use a hose to disperse black and whitefly on your broad beans. *Anna Ingram, Professional Horticulturalist*

Keep a spray bottle of soapy water in the kitchen garden so you are ready to spray green and blackfly the minute they arrive on your veg – wash the veg before eating! *Sara Stonor, Vice Lord-Lieutenant, E. Sussex and also from Richard Jackman,*

If your plants get covered in aphids, be patient and brave! Hoverflies, ladybirds and birds will come and feast on them once their numbers are high enough! However, if you spray pesticides or even use soap and water to get rid of them the food web will not develop sufficiently to deal with your pests and you will always have to be spraying them, and the whole ecosystem suffers. *Imogen Jackson, Head Gardener, horticultural therapist, Horatio's Garden, Midlands*

To repel the dreaded lily beetle on your precious lilies as they grow, spray with a solution of mashed raw garlic (2 cloves) that has been steeped in 1 litre boiling water and cooled. Spray regularly, but avoid beneficial insects. *Francine Raymond, Garden Writer*

The first lily beetles coming out of underground hibernation in early spring are often to be found (and can be therefore be nobbled) cutting their teeth on your fritillaries. *Helen Yemm, Daily Telegraph Columnist & Author of 'Gardening in Pyjamas'*

Sow hardy annual flowers and many vegetables into cell trays first. This ensures they are easier to keep watered and not so readily eaten by slugs and can be planted in patterns or rows where you want them. *Simon Newman, Professional Gardener*

Avoid direct-sowing slug-prone veg. Sow batches of seed in 9cm pots. Prick out individually into 9cm pots and then transplant into the veg beds when 10cm high. This seems to cut down on slug damage and the plants get away better. *Ellie Cochrane*

Companion Planting to keep the bugs down!

This summer I started growing vegetables amongst flowers and I have had great success with chillies and peppers in large pots with geraniums around them. I realised that not only does it look beautiful but the geraniums keep the bugs away. *Kara Rawden*

Garlic planted under a rose helps keep black spot at bay.
Anne Hawkins

Grow *Tagetes* (French Marigolds) as companion plants to your greenhouse tomatoes, to deter whitefly infestations. Although *Tagetes'* distinctive scent isn't liked by whitefly, the human nose thinks otherwise. *Carlyn Kilpatrick, Horticultural Therapist, The Nurture Project*

Plant marigolds here and there, they deter insects.
Dame Helen Mirren

Plant *Tagetes* or basil beside tomatoes in your greenhouse to discourage whitefly. *Richard & Sandy Roff*

Create a suitably-sized gap in your fences or garden gate to allow hedgehogs into your garden. They will help keep your slug and snail population under control. Please don't put slug pellets round your plants. *Sue Stirling*

Chickens are great for keeping your bug population down. We have fabulous chickens of our own who roam around our vegetable garden. *Sophie Allport, www.sophieallport.com*

If you keep hens, choose a house on legs. This will make it easier to clean out at waist level, make the space below usable as a dust bath and you'll be able to check there are no undesirable residents squatting underneath. *Francine Raymond, Garden Writer*

If you lift your dahlias over winter, sprinkle them with some chilli powder as it helps stop mice nibbling at the tubers. *Petra Venton*

To stop mice eating pea and bean seeds, soak them in liquid seaweed – it disguises the smell. *Stephanie Donaldson*

Rabbits: having tried everything to protect our garden the best way I've found is to make this concoction! Steep chilli flakes and garlic in warm water & milk for several days. Then sieve it into a spray bottle & start spraying the plants. You will need to re-apply the spray regularly but it does deter rabbits munching. *Mark Lane, Broadcaster, Writer, Garden Designer*

Dahlias are my favourite flower, unfortunately the slugs and snails seem to like them too. I have found the best way to protect them is to surround them with a ring of grit – all the way round and at least 10cm wide. They won't like to crawl over it. This will work for other plants such as lupins. *Nicki Conlon*

In dry weather hunt for gangs of crustily snoozing snails lurking in stacks of old flowerpots and other dry places, (including those going it alone aloft on trellises, the shady side of drain pipes and on the branches of shrubs). *Helen Yemm*

To stop the slugs eating the plants in your pots (especially hostas, loved by slugs) smear Vaseline on the rim of the pots. *Gill Mullin and also from Joy Moore*

...Or save your old filter-coffee granules and use them to cover the soil around your hostas. Apply quite a thick layer to deter the slugs. *Heidi*

If you are bothered by cats digging in newly dug soil or compost. Place lots of small twigs and sticks end up in the soil to stop the cats. Avoids using chemicals too. *Nicola Macnee*

If you have pigeons/cats around cover rows of vegetable seeds with nets to keep the pigeons/cats off until the seedlings are well grown. *Julia Collard*

Take care what you buy from garden centres. Even 'RHS recommended' plants for pollinators may be treated with pesticides during propagation and you may be attracting insects only to kill them. *Isabella Tree, Knepp Rewilding Project*

Research the various pests and diseases and help others in identifying issues. *Kevin Fortey, Guinness World Record Holder for the World's Heaviest Beetroot weighing 23.995kg*

Hygiene is an important aspect in gardening. Try and create an ambience suitable for your planting. Encourage natural predators i.e. ladybirds, hover fly larvae, parasitic wasps and beetles, earwigs etc by not using chemicals and encouraging wildlife into your garden. *Anna Ingram*

NOTES & OBSERVATIONS

----

11. THE BIRDS & THE BEES

Look after your garden workforce. Provide bird boxes, berried shrubs and shelter. Ensure there is water in a ground level shallow bowl with a few stones to allow hedgehogs and bees to drink and birds to bath. *Rozanne Delamore*

Different bird-box styles suit different birds. There is plenty of advice on the RSPB web site. For instance, by attracting blue tits to nest you'll also take advantage of the natural pest control they provide, collecting caterpillars and pests from around your garden to feed their hungry chicks. *Adam Pasco, former Editor of BBC Gardener's World Magazine*

Keep some dense thorny habitat if you can (a corner of brambles, nettles, scrubby patch for wildlife) – the only reason to buy a birdbox is if you're not providing natural bird-nesting habitat elsewhere. *Isabella Tree, Author of 'Wilding' and co-owner of the Knepp Re-Wilding Project*

Try to keep a part of your garden 'wild' – the invertebrates that hedgehogs and amphibians rely on for food thrive in damp and overgrown places – so do not over tidy things.
Dave Risley, Folly Wildlife Rescue Trust

Hedgehogs will often construct their nests beneath bushes and shrubs – so garden with care! *Dave Risley*

Many hedgehogs, amphibians and slow worms are injured by strimmers, so check long grass before you commence work – it could save a life. *Dave Risley*

Do not buy remote lawn mowers – they kill hedgehogs.
Susan Bowie

Allow small corridors – a gap at the base of a fence panel to allow
hedgehogs to pass through. They are not only a gardener's great
friend but in danger themselves as they could starve in just
one garden. *Philip Bailey*

Ensure ponds and swimming pools have a slope or escape ramp –
many hedgehogs drown when they can't get out. *Dave Risley*

Consider planting flowers in your garden or allotment to attract
bees, butterflies and other pollinators or build a bee hotel.
Stevan, Eastleigh Borough and Romsey MENCAP Gardening Club

Keep in mind non-hibernating bees in winter and provide nectar
loving winter flowering plants. *Hilary O'Donnell Cam*

Bee and butterfly shallow water stations are a must in a garden.
If you have a pond, create a shallow end with layers of stones for
drinking and cooling down. *Hilary O'Donnell Cam*

Nettles are food plants for many butterfly species. The caterpillars
of Comma, Peacock, Red Admiral, and Tortoiseshell butterflies,
all feed on nettles. Nettles are also an important food plant for
the caterpillars of many moths. So, if you want to help butterflies
and moths, nettles are well worth including in your garden!
Beth Otway, Horticulturalist & Garden Writer

Keep a certain amount of comfrey in the garden. It is the feed plant for Garden Tiger Moth Caterpillars. *Lady Sandwich*

Plant buddleias and watch the butterflies dance. *Sue Rowles*

Plant only native plants – perennials that are pollinator friendly and add biodiversity to local eco-systems. *Barbara Passero*

Old walls and crumbling masonry and woodwork are great for bats and insects so don't renovate everything at once. *Isabella Tree*

Reduce or get rid of outside lights that may be deterring or killing night-time moths (night-time moths are more important pollinators than bees) and disorientating bats. *Isabella Tree*

Buy a pair of binoculars and some wildlife guide books!
Isabella Tree

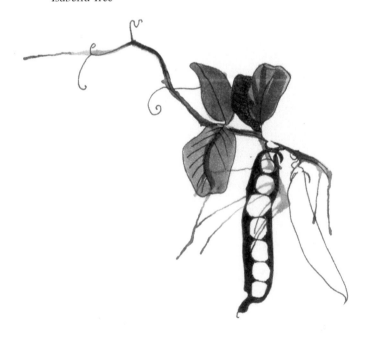

All gardens could be wilder, more naturalistic, more biologically diverse and wildlife friendly. *Michael Walker, National Gardens Specialist*

Don't tidy up too much, let your hair down! Use no chemicals. *Isabella Tree, co-owner of the Knepp Project, W. Sussex, author of 'Wilding'.*

Why not stop mowing some of your lawn for the month of May? You might be amazed at the native flowers that could appear given the chance. We were thrilled this year to see wild orchids growing in our garden, little pink pyramids coming up where the grass was left unmown. *Justin Welby, Archbishop of Canterbury*

Wild Flower Meadows

- Start small, it is far easier to prepare the ground, sow and manage a smaller area than taking on a whole field. You can always enlarge it as you become more confident.
- Start collecting seeds whilst out walking anytime from late Spring onwards. Make sure the seeds are kept dry until ready to sow.
- Hire a turf cutter and remove top layer, at least 10-15cm. Import the poorest quality soil you can source.
- Sow your seeds early Autumn and wait for the magic to begin.
- Once flowering is over the following year, cut the meadow (early September) and allow to dry out and for any seeds to self-sow.
- October onwards rake away.
- Good luck, the butterflies will thank you.
  Amanda Garratt

Set Yourself and Your Lawn Free

During this year's covid-19 isolation period I noticed an abundance of bees and butterflies. And it got me thinking, what if we set the lawn free and wild it. It turned out to be a brilliant idea! Wild flora soon popped through the beautifully kept lawn, we cut paths wide enough to walk on. The first thing to appear was clover that had been sitting in wait for a life time and what a magnificent display, soon followed by bugle (*Lamiaceae*) leaving small puddles of blue. And of course sprinkles of white and yellow in buttercups and daisies. Patches of birds-foot-trefoil, speedwell and finally ox-eye daisy. In all it was the best decision because not only did the insects enjoy it, I did too. The lawn has now been cut ready for next year and I'm really looking forward to seeing what else pops up. Have a go you'll be astonished. Happy wilding, *Jeff Beck*

If your neighbours give you grief about how untidy your garden looks, join the Blue Campaign – plant a blue heart in your garden to show them you know what you're doing. Perhaps your ideas will catch on, and then your neighbours will get one. And then the only person in the street who looks out of place is the one whose garden is sterile and manicured. *Isabella Tree*

If you have a large garden with a big lawn, consider leaving a section to just 'do its thing'! You will be surprised at how many different grasses and plants appear and it is a haven for wildlife. I once heard a garden lawn described as a green desert and they were right. I have gotten so much satisfaction from the unmown area of our garden, listening to the grasshoppers and watching all the insects that now call it home. *Zec Richardson*

Learn to stop over-gardening. Take a tiny section of garden,
50cm x 50cm or more. Remove all plants, grass, weeds until
all that is left is bare soil. For the next few years watch it closely.
Things will start to grow in that soil of their own accord. If anything
becomes too dominant, remove it entirely or in part. Keep watching
and editing. Over time, so much can be learnt about the nature of
a garden, about how plants travel and grow and can be managed.
*Lisbet Rausing, Nicky Browne, Head Gardener, Wadhurst Park and
Sara Jackson, Gardener, Rolf's Farm*

Grass is the dominant factor in a wildflower meadow. To succeed
you will need to strip the ground of nutrients, rake and rake until
you see bare ground, include Yellow Rattle (*Rhinanthus minor*) which
is semi-parasitic to suppress the grass. If possible, sow your seeds in
the autumn, if not in the spring and then sit back and watch your
meadow grow!! Leave the plants to die back naturally at the end of
summer and naturally disperse seeds and then you can rake the area
clear of debris. *Anna Ingram, Horticulturist*

'Yellow Rattle' (*Rhinanthus minor*) keeps the grass from
dominating and lets meadow plants flower their hearts out'
Tom Cutter, Senior Gardener at Glendurgan Garden

Biodiversity is the key to life, the foundation of a happy garden.
Stephen Mason Community Gardener.

The most useful tip I can give is work with nature – do not try and
fight it by using sprays or chemicals. You will get greater results and
satisfaction than you could imagine. *Philip Bailey*

13. TOO MANY VEG?

A selection of recipes for when your garden has been just too, too productive!

TOMATO JAM

Ingredients:
1kg ripe tomatoes.
$^1/_2$ cup of dark brown sugar
2 tbsp apple cider vinegar
1 tbsp grated ginger
4 fat cloves of garlic
1 tsp kosher salt
$^1/_2$ tsp ground cumin
$^1/_4$ tsp smoked paprika
$^1/_4$ tsp red pepper flakes
$^1/_4$ tsp red chilli flakes
The grated zest & juice of 1 unwaxed lemon

Method:
- Blitz the garlic and ginger in a food processor, then add $^1/_4$ of the tomatoes and blitz briefly again to a rough texture. Place in preserving pan.
- Roughly chop remaining tomatoes and add to pan with all the other ingredients; stir well to mix. Bring slowly to the boil and simmer for approximately 2 hours until it has reduced and is thick and jammy.
- Spoon while hot into sterilised jars and seal immediately. I usually water bath as well to ensure a good seal. Keeps for several months in a dark place.

Makes approx. 2 x 400ml jars or 3-4 smaller ones.
Sent by Helen Lawson

RUNNER BEAN CHUTNEY

If you have a glut of runner beans, enjoy them all year round in a delicious chutney from Nigel Slater.

Ingredients:
2 medium onions
150ml malt vinegar
8 allspice berries
1 tsp coriander seeds
1 tsp yellow mustard seed
750g runner beans,
1 tbsp English mustard powder
2tsp grain mustard
2 tsp turmeric
150ml cider vinegar
1 heaped tsp salt
250g tomatoes
28g cornflour
200g granulated sugar

Method:
- Peel and chop onions, put in medium saucepan with malt vinegar, allspice, coriander and mustard seeds.
- Bring to boil, then simmer 10 minutes.
- String the beans, slice thinly diagonally. Cook beans in pan of boiling water for 1 minute.
- Mix mustards, turmeric, sugar, salt and half cider vinegar in a bowl.
- Dice tomatoes and add to this with remaining cider vinegar, beans and mustard mixture. Simmer for 15 minutes.
- The beans should be tender but still bright.

CONTINUED OVER

- Remove $2/3$ tbsps. liquid and mix with cornflour to a paste. Stir into mixture and allow to simmer and thicken for a minute or two.
- Ladle into warm, sterile jars and seal.
  Sent by Anne F

RUNNER-BEANS THAT ARE TOO OLD TO EAT!

Don't compost them. These are still good to eat when green. Shell them, then plunge the beans into boiling salted water. Boil them for 10 minutes.

Runner beans, like most beans, contain toxins (poisons). Boiling them for 10 minutes breaks down the toxins. They are no longer harmful but very good to eat.

Pop them into your favourite home-made sauce and enjoy them hot or cold. *Sent by Myra Sealy*

COURGETTE CAKE

Courgette glut? I highly recommend you make a deliciously moist, rich, velvety chocolate courgette cake.

Ingredients
350g self-raising flour
50g cocoa powder
1 tsp mixed spice or cinnamon
175ml olive oil
375g golden caster sugar

3 eggs
2 tsp vanilla extract
500ml grated courgette (about 2 medium courgettes)

Icing
200g dark chocolate chopped
100ml double cream
Or keep it simple and just mix icing sugar and cocoa powder
together to top cake.

Method:

- Heat the oven to 180°C/160°C fan/gas 4. In a large bowl, combine the flour, cocoa powder, mixed spice/cinnamon.
- In another bowl, combine the olive oil, sugar, eggs, vanilla essence and grated courgette.
- Mix the dry and wet mixture until just combined.
- Line a 24cm cake tin with greaseproof paper, then pour in your mixture. Bake for about 40-50 minutes or until a knife inserted into the middle comes out clean.
- Cool in the tin for 10 minutes, then turn out onto a wire rack and leave to cool.
- Grab a cup of tea, slice and enjoy!
  Sent by Debi Holland

VEGAN COURGETTE CAKE WITH LEMON GLAZE

Ingredients
2 medium courgettes (approx. 350g)
finely grated zest of 2 lemons
100g light brown soft sugar
80g caster sugar

CONTINUED OVER

120ml sunflower oil
60ml unsweetened non-dairy milk
60ml lemon juice
260g plain flour
1 tsp baking powder
$^{1}/_{2}$ tsp bicarbonate of soda
2 tsps spice of your choice, e.g. nutmeg, cinnamon
$^{1}/_{2}$ tsp salt

Lemon Glaze:
85g icing sugar
juice of $^{1}/_{2}$ lemon

Method:

- Preheat the oven to 180°C/350F/gas mark 4. Grease a loaf tin (11.5 x 21.5 cm) and line with a strip of baking parchment. Make sure that you leave some overhanging on either side so that you can lift the cake out easily.
- Coarsely grate the courgette and place the grated flesh in a clean tea towel over the sink. Firmly squeeze out most of the excess water.
- Place the grated courgette in a large bowl along with the lemon zest, light brown soft sugar, caster sugar, sunflower oil, milk and lemon juice.
- Whisk until well combined.
- Add the flour, baking powder, bicarbonate of soda, spices and salt. Stir until no dry lumps remain.
- Working quickly, tip the batter into the prepared loaf tin, spread it level and place in the preheated oven.

- Bake for about 70 minutes until a skewer inserted into the centre comes out clean. Leave to cool in the tin.
- Once the cake is cool, sift the icing sugar into a bowl and gradually stir in the lemon juice until you have a thick but pourable glaze.
- Drizzle the glaze over the top of the cake and serve.
  Sent by James Warham

COURGETTE PIE

Ingredients
For the filling:
4 large courgettes
1 small handful of parsley, mint & dill, all finely chopped
250g cheese (e.g. feta, grated cheddar)
4 eggs
$^{1}/_{2}$ tsp nutmeg
Olive Oil, for brushing
Salt & Pepper for seasoning

For the filo pastry (alternatively, buy the filo pastry ready-made)
250g plain flour
$^{1}/_{2}$ tsp salt
30ml olive oil
$^{1}/_{2}$ tsp white-wine vinegar
Flour, for dusting

CONTINUED OVER

Method:

- Cut off the ends of the courgettes and grate into a large colander (no need to peel them). Allow to rest.
- To make the filo dough:
- Place the flour in a bowl with the salt. Make a well in the centre and pour in the olive oil and vinegar. Start mixing, either with a spoon or your hands, adding lukewarm water until it resembles a soft dough. You will need approximately 125ml of water. Tip the dough onto a floured surface and knead lightly until smooth then place it back in the bowl and cover with a tea towel. Allow to rest for 1 hour.
- Preheat the oven to 180°C, 160°C fan/gas mark 4.
- Squeeze out any remaining liquid from the courgette and place in a bowl. Add the herbs, cheeses and eggs, mixing well with a wooden spoon. Season with salt and pepper and nutmeg.
- Brush a 20cm round baking tray with oil. Transfer the dough to a surface that has been dusted with flour. Divide the dough into 3 balls. Take 1 ball of dough and roll out into a dinner-plate sized round. Brush with some olive oil and set aside. Roll out another piece of dough to the same size and place on top of the oiled piece, then brush with oil. Repeat with the third piece of dough. You will have 3 sheets that have been oiled in between.
- Roll these together and lay the dough on the baking tray. Spoon the filling into the middle of the dough, leaving a large border. Fold the edges of the dough over part of the filling, crimping as you go around. Brush the edges with a little olive oil and bake for about 30 minutes or until the dough is golden and the filling is firm.
- Serve at room temperature.
  Sent by Jenifer Morley

CHARRED COURGETTE WITH LEMON, OREGANO & CHILLI FLAKES

Ingredients;
4 courgettes
Olive oil
2 tbsp wild oregano
1 tsp chilli flakes
Seasoning
Juice of $1/2$ lemon
Cherry tomatoes, to decorate

Method:
- Preheat the oven to its highest setting. Line a baking tray with baking paper.
- Cut the courgettes diagonally into 1cm-thick slices and spread them out onto the baking tray. Drizzle generously with olive oil and sprinkle over all the remaining dry ingredients (not the lemon juice). Season with salt and pepper.
- Roast the courgettes in the oven for 8 minutes then remove, squeeze the lemon juice over them, then roast for a further 6 minutes.
- Arrange on plate and decorate with cherry tomatoes.
  Sent by: Jenifer Morley

COURGETTE BRUSCHETTA

Ingredients
4 courgettes, washed and trimmed
about 4 tbsp olive oil
1 tsp rosemary, oregano or marjoram leaves, finely chopped
4 large or 8 small (e.g. baguette size) slices chewy textured white bread
1 garlic clove, peeled
50g Parmesan, flaked or shaved
salt and pepper

Method:
- Slice the courgettes into ribbons using a vegetable peeler, cutting lengthways down the courgettes. Brush each slice very sparingly with olive oil.
- Heat a frying pan until very hot. Fry the courgettes slices in batches, turning so that both sides have a few brown spots or stripes
- Try not to overcook the courgette ribbons though, they are nice if they keep a bit of juiciness. Once all the slices are cooked, sprinkle with salt and pepper and toss the herbs through.
- To make the bruschetta, toast both sides of the bread. Rub one side of the toasted bread lightly with the garlic clove, followed by a trickle of olive oil.
- Pile the chargrilled courgettes onto the bruschetta, add a few more drops of olive oil and the chilli slivers if using. Finish with a few flakes of Parmesan and serve.

Sent by Rosie Kefford

TOO MANY GREENGAGES
OR DAMSONS?

Pickle them!

Ingredients:
2 kg greengages… halved and stoned
1 litre white distilled vinegar
500g granulated or caster sugar
seeds of 20 cardamom pods
2 tbsps. green peppercorns
5g mace blades
12 dried red chillies

Method:
- Pack the gages into 4 x $^1/_2$ litre sterilized preserving jars.
- Boil the vinegar and sugar, stirring, until the sugar
  has dissolved.
- Pour onto gages in the jars, turn jars upside down for
  15 minutes or so to seal lids.
- Store in a cool place for up to six months.
  Sent by Anne F

TOO MUCH SQUASH...

I pick, cut up and boil any extra squash I have. I put the cooking liquid (chicken broth or water) and the squash in a container after cooking and freeze. When it is soup season I thaw squash and puree for soup stock. *Ilena Gilbert-Mays, North Carolina, US*

Often, squashes and pumpkins are too big for one meal. So take the time to remove the skin from them, remove the seeds and dice into inch cubes. Brush with good olive oil and roast for 20 minutes at about 180°C. Cool and portion up, label the bags and freeze. I find it so useful to get a bag out of the freezer, defrost and add to a curry or to roasted vegetables. *Anna Matthews*

TOO MUCH ANYTHING

Soups made from any vegetable glut, especially spinach or courgette, can be stored in the freezer and enjoyed on a cold winter's day. Lettuce which is looking as if it will bolt can also be used in the same way. *Julie Comet*

KEEP IT FRESH!

Keep your chilli crop really fresh by freezing them in a plastic bag. Simply take them out when you need them. *Anne F*

AND DELICIOUS...

Best way to prepare sweet corn. First: steam don't boil! Second: serve with sea salt, chili, and lime. Simply divine! *Charlotte Blome*

14. THE FINAL FARRAGO
MUSINGS & TIMESAVERS

PRACTICALITIES AND TIME SAVERS

Get up an hour earlier. It's amazing what you can achieve when you are not being pestered. *Ellie Cochrane*

Always plan ahead, check weather, allow yourself time to get things done. *Alexander McCallum, Gardener, Miserden Estate.*

Diarise the work for good weather, if the work gets forgotten or late it can affect results. *Susan Young, Susan Young Garden Design*

Pay attention. Things can go wrong very quickly, so check leaves constantly for weaknesses, and feed or mulch the plant accordingly. Bugs have a very good understanding of a weakened plant and take advantage. *Dame Helen Mirren*

Divide the jobs that need doing up into smaller manageable tasks. I set myself a few tasks per week and keep them small to lessen the impact it will have and hopefully avoid a flare up. *Zec Richardson*

Start the day with a job that is simple and needs doing. Jobs like edging the lawn, this will get you around the garden in which time you can look at and think about what else needs doing for the rest of the day. *Barty Meredith-Hardy, Professional Gardener*

Remember that sometimes 'doing nothing' can be as hard as 'doing a lot'. As a gardener you always feel the need to improve a space. However, it is important to recognise when little or nothing is needed and to gently manage what nature is already doing well enough. Take photos through the year and really look, don't just plan. *Louis Adlington, Sole Gardener, Private Estate.*

Spread yourself thin covering everything rather than staying on one job too long. *Alexander McCallum*

A little often is better than loads later. *Anne Hawkins*

if you're short of time and want to spruce up your garden, ...mow the lawn and trim the lawn edges to give the garden an instant lift. *Anita Foy Garden designer*

or simply... edge and deadhead. *Petra Venton*

Deadheading especially worthwhile for lengthening flowering times on lupins, cosmos, dahlias. *Jane Guy*

and remember: hedges & edges – If your garden is getting out of control, concentrate on the grass, edges and fronts of beds and hedges. *Susan Bowie*

Don't allow gardening to overwhelm you. Focus on one area at a time and know that all gardeners make mistakes or are not always successful in their plant growing. If you think you haven't got green fingers you just haven't tried enough times! *Imogen Jackson, Head Gardener, horticultural therapist, Horatio's Garden, Midlands*

Women's nylon tights make perfect plant ties, Cut the tights into loops so they look like slices of calamari then use these loops to tie in roses, stems to stakes or bunch bulb foliage together. They are incredibly soft so do not crush stems but at the same time incredibly strong and will not break without being cut. *Debi Holland*

Slip a square of kitchen roll in your pocket instead of a tissue. It won't disintegrate in the damp the way that tissues do. *Gill Mullin*

A scaffold board is very useful in the vegetable garden - you can stand on it so the soil doesn't get compacted and use it as a straight line to make sure you have straight rows of seeds. *Alex*

Cut down on weeding, use groundcover such as hardy geraniums, vinca or hardy herbs to cover bare soil and smother weeds. *Debi Holland*

Don't tidy up too much – let your hair down! *Isabella Tree, Knepp Re-Wilding Project*

I believe, it was Sir Geoffrey Jellicoe, who said words to the effect that… 'Gardens were the only art form that changes through time'. So do not worry if you get something wrong, or something dies. You are just changing the art that is your garden. *Robert Brett, Curator, RHS Garden Hyde Hall*

When using a wheelbarrow, always set it down pointing in the direction of travel. So that when you pick it back up again, and it is loaded, you do not have any difficult U-turn manoeuvres to complete... *Dean Peckett Head of Horticulture, Arne Maynard Garden Design*

When moving large amounts of organic matter with shovel and wheelbarrow – slow and steady wins the day, just keep going backwards and forwards and eventually it will all be shifted. Do not over fill the wheelbarrow as the excess will spill over the side. *Barty Meredith-Hardy*

My Granddad, born in the 1890s, always said: "The best manure is the sole of the farmer's boot". He meant that if you look round your patch every day you would see what was going wrong before it got too bad – some pests arriving, a damaged fence, rabbits digging or some ailment starting in your leek bed. He was born on a farm in Dorset but moved to London, where his garden in Chingford was full of fruit and vegetables, including espaliered apple and pear trees. I remember this tip all the time. *Rosalind Riley*

Practicalities – Stay Well!

Use lots of high factor sunscreen even if it is cloudy.
Barty Meredith-Hardy

Make sure you get a tetanus shot. *Charlotte Blome*

Do a few gentle stretches before starting to do lots of digging or heavy work, and yoga exercises are great for keeping you supple and to ease aching backs. *Michael Brown, Garden Historian*

When I had a bad back, a friend advised me to work in short shifts. I did 15 minutes a time, just weeding a few square feet, then carrying no more than a trug of manure or garden compost to cover the area. I really got to know my garden, the garden looked great after a few months and it gave me confidence to learn more. *Alexandra Campbell*

So you forgot to wear your gloves and now your fingernails are stained. Don't fret! Just rub the stains with half a lemon and watch them disappear! *Charlotte Blome*

Herbs can help: lemon balm may uplift the spirit and calm nevous exhaustion, and could be used to treat stress headaches and migraines: thyme may calm stomach problems and soothe a sore throat: lavender is great before bed to help with insomnia! *Vanessa Austin*

Do it your way!

if you are right handed work from right to left, when weeding, pruning, hedge-cutting, so your working hand is close to the job and not reaching across your body. The opposite applies if you are left handed. I've found this makes the job flow smoother and you get more done with less fatigue. *Simon Newman, Professional Gardener*

Everyone has their own way to garden, find what suits you best and make it your own. *Alexander McCallum*

If you have an area and you can't decide what to do with it, cover it up with cardboard / carpet or Mypex until you have made your mind up. That way, when you have decided what you want to do with it, you have a weed-free, blank canvas to work with! No-dig simplicity at its finest! *Blooming Green Flowers*

Young children love to dig for worms, older ones for potatoes. *Anne Hawkins*

Don't forget to stand back and look at what you are doing from a few different viewpoints at regular intervals. It will help keep work like pruning a shrub in its context. *Barty Meredith-Hardy*

Do what gives you joy and happiness. *Jeremy Homewood, Bumbles Plant Centre*

Labelling & Recording

Always record the name of the plant, tree or shrub in a book and note where you planted it. This helps if you lose the label. *Christine Walkden, Horticulturist*

Use a pencil to write plant names on labels. This seems to last longer than using "permanent" ink. *Richard & Sandy Roff*

Label EVERYTHING... you will forget what they are. That applies to seeds you sow in a pot, or parsnip soup you put in the freezer that you made from that glut of parsnips and it turns out to be apple puree when you take it back out. *Anna Matthews, Sole Gardener, Private Estate*

When I am in my potting shed I always make sure I have all the compost and seeds in buckets nearby with a small plastic scoop, labels and a pencil. *Lady Arabella Lennox-Boyd, Garden Designer*

Keep a notebook strictly for gardening. Anything new or insightful you have learned, add it. Take stock of what doesn't work well in a garden and write it down. Draw and sketch what is inspiring you. Sometimes those moments are so fleeting that it's important to capture them when you can, so much of our incredible design comes from subconscious ideas. *Brandon George*

Keep a camera/your phone with you when gardening so you can photo what things look like when they're not in season.
Anna Matthews

Enjoy! ...it's good for you!

DO NOT forget to walk round your garden and enjoy it. If you are a gardenaholic, it is very easy to spot what needs doing and not to stop and admire. *Sue Rowles*

Don't stress if it all goes wrong! *Ann Wells*

Activities that allow you to enter a highly-focussed state of mind of 'flow' are rated as highly relaxing by many gardeners. Such activities include weeding, watering, deadheading, pottering about, and observing the garden. When you are in the zone, nothing else seems to matter! Having said this, any aspect of gardening can provide a particular delight to individuals. *Dr Lauriane Chalmin-Pui, Wellbeing Researcher, RHS*

Soil contains *Mycobacterium vaccae*, which releases natural anti-depressants serotonin and dopamine so getting our hands dirty can genuinely improve our mental health and make us feel more positive. *Debi Holland*

The garden is still a riot of colour in September and will go on until much later thanks to ruthless planting and dead heading. If something becomes a thug or doesn't have a long flowering gardening season out it goes to friends with larger gardens. *Paula Bolton, Jewellery Designer to the RHS*

Slow down, stop, and really focus on exactly how one plant looks, feels or smells. Take time to really study it and get to know it well. Watch your insects. Get to know them and their habits- they are fascinating! You may well find you feel much calmer after just watching. *Imogen Jackson*

Take time to enjoy your garden. Even if it's just a few minutes a day and its dark by the time you get out there. *Anna Matthews*

Don't be afraid to experiment in the garden and make mistakes. It's so important to have fun and try things out - some plants will do well and some won't! Learning from nature - and mistakes made along the way - are an essential part of gardening success. Enjoy it! *Katie Vanstone, Gardener, Fursdon House, Devon*

When you have done what you can in the garden – relax! Enjoy the garden for what it is and for what it will become. This 'letting go' brings unexpected benefits to both the gardener and the natural world. Don't mind the 'weeds' when they arrive, they are gifts from the wild – dandelions, cow parsley, sow thistle and more grace my garden, and they call in more bees and butterflies than the cultivated plants. Enjoy! *Anni Kelsey*

When bits of you ache and your finger nails are rimed with earth and you're thinking of giving up and getting an indoor plant instead - don't! Make yourself a cup of tea (with a chocolate biscuit), sit down and look at what YOU'VE achieved in YOUR garden. Marvellous! *Susan MacCulloch*

Nothing is ever impossible, set your gardening goal and then find a way to achieve it. Sometimes the challenge of adapting your garden, beds or planters or a tool can be as rewarding as the activity itself. There will always be a way round a problem, gardening doesn't discriminate, it's open to all. *Andy Wright, Therapeutic Gardens Manager*

Most importantly sit down and watch your garden grow. *Michelle*

During each season, winter, spring, summer and autumn, aim to venture out into the garden at sunrise or sunset on at least 2 or 3 occasions. Each season brings its own unique sensory experience and this is enhanced during the times of dawn and dusk. This is when the garden awakens during those first rays of sunshine or when the garden becomes still and twilight fades. It only lasts a few minutes but every second during that brief moment is unique, filled with sights, sounds, feeling and fragrance. *Dean Peckett, Head of Horticulture at Arne Maynard*

We may not all have gardens, but all of us CAN grow! Be it a basil plant within an empty bean tin, into which you've punched a few holes, or a recycled tray that fruit was delivered in and repurposed as a seed tray for a selection of micro-herbs or salad leaves, if you've a windowsill, you can grow! *Simon Lycett, Celebrity Floral Designer*

A garden is always a work in progress – it's never finished. *Alan Titchmarsh*

Thoughts on Gardening as the years mature

When one's power of sight is changing
Into darkness like the night,
There still drifts fragrance from the flowers
To whoever waits and wanders through my gate.

I now no longer really threaten weeds,
Bending, crawling, kneeling, or ignoring them.
I've come to speak of weeds
As things being decorative "en masse"
And "natural" wherever they chose to congregate.
John Dudgeon

For many years my gardening was only several window boxes on a balcony in SW10, in London, so coming down to a real garden in Somerset was quite a surprise and clearly takes up much more time and effort. Though where I am now is not very large and what's more, I am not particularly knowledgeable, I know what I like to see in my garden - plants that grow upwards towards the sun, are colourful and most importantly, dead-head easily and are not too popular with the dreaded slugs!

This year I have planted a profusion of brightly coloured gazanias, which keep flowering when dead-headed.
Valerie Singleton OBE

Slow(er) Gardening
In the curious summer of 2020

Take time – to take an early morning stroll, maybe secateurs in hand
Take time – to see which plants are thriving, are happy with their
　　　　　neighbours, or struggling, or thirsty
Take time – to list new plants and ideas for next year
Take time – to take an evening stroll, watering can to hand
Take time – to stand and stare.
Richard Stileman

Historically, men were the gardeners. Their 'bottom-of-the-garden sheds' were sacrosanct. The loss of so many men in World War 1 brought women into the game. For the first time 'bloomers'(!) were seen at Kew! World War 2 saw women in the Land Army doing a full day's work on the farm. Tools were created for men, not women and women struggled with the weight and size. *Heather Fooks*

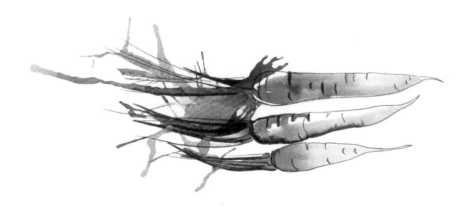

Final Thoughts

The process of gardening is its purpose. *Sir Charles Fraser*

Let the garden talk to you, not the other way around. *Marie Cornish*

Should I weed the lawn or say it's a garden? *Graham Peters*

"He that planteth a tree is a servant of God, he provideth a kindness for many generations, and faces that he hath not seen shall bless him." Henry Van Dyke sent by *Graham Peters*

A TASTE OF PROVENCE IN SUSSEX

When we moved to the Downland village of Bishopstone over 20 years ago, we were told by an older resident that after the 14 June or thereabouts, the free draining, alkaline chalk gardens of our village struggle to keep shape and colour for the rest of the summer. The obvious answer is mulch and more mulch, but if you haven't the time or energy for that, what are the best reliable plants and trees to grow in a Downland chalk garden in a hot summer without too much effort or trouble?

Firstly, consider the herb families and think topiary to get architectural shape to a drooping garden. Rosemary can be trained into a topiary half standard, as can bay and lavender be trained into hedges and topiary balls. Lavender is a must for our garden. One of our village neighbours grew lavender for sale here for a while with infinite varieties. The most successful is probably English lavender in its various cultivars. Hidcote is good for hedging. Rosea grows here as well with its unique pink flowers and green leaves. Munstead is another good variety with a bright blue flower. Spanish and French varieties can be grown here but local frost pockets and proximity to sea salt make them more vulnerable in our experience. Secondly, the wonderful sage or salvia family grow well throughout and late into the summer with infinite varieties (but stick to the hardy ones if possible), with all kinds of scents, colours and shapes – not just the popular Hot Lips variety either! The lovely Sierra San Antonia, pink and flamboyant and Salvia Javier, blue and dramatic, like the dry conditions, as does the red Silas Dyson variety – very hardy indeed. Not all salvias survive the winter, but fortunately even average gardeners like us are able to take cuttings that will survive and thrive. Thirdly, the reliable *Verbascum Thapsus*, a tall graceful (6 feet if lucky) spike of elegant yellow flowers gives height and interesting grey leaves in the hottest summer unwatered!

Coastal chalk gardens have also some late summer treats worth cultivating that benefit from the dry conditions. An archaeological dig discovered the Saxons latrines on our village green, were full of evidence of fig eating. They were not imported but grown here! Indeed, the Victorians grew figs on this fringe of the coast in special Fig Picnic Gardens and to this day we have abundant crops especially green figs. Figs love the impoverished dry soil and if you constrict their roots while planting, they will reward you with big crops at least every other year.

Grapes flourish if pruned properly (ours are not). Olive trees grow well in sheltered areas and give elegant height, and we have also grown kiwi on a south facing flint wall, albeit with more flowers than fruit. All in all, a South Coast late summer chalk garden can look positively Provencal after the cottage garden colours of the mid-June garden are burnt away by the Sussex sun.
David & Karen Allam

5-a month! Gardening Tasks to take you through the year from
John Richardson, Johnson's of Whixley

January
1) Clean rainwater gutters from all buildings to prevent spring
overflows. 2) In freezing conditions ensure the ice on the pond is
broken to allow the escape of toxic gases and oxygen exchange.
Do not hammer the ice as it may stun the fish. 3) Service the
lawnmower, the grass will be growing again very soon! 4) If there
is heavy snowfall, brush snow off conifers and heathers to prevent
damage. 5) Turn compost heaps top to bottom and sides to the
middle for even degrading.

February
1) Repair broken spouts, fences, trellises, steps, and walls. Clean
out & sterilise bird boxes. 2) Divide and replant snowdrops as the
flowers go over. 3) Prune climbing roses, keep 5-7 strong shoots and
cut others back to within 3 buds of the base. 4) Prune shrub roses
late February to encourage growth from the base. Remove some
old shoots. 5) Complete formative pruning of trees and shrubs,
remove leader if a bush form is required.

March
1) Dig potato trenches incorporating well-rotted manure into the
trench base. 2) Prune decorative Cornus and Salix to within 5cm
of old shoots. Prune 'Midwinter Fire' lightly. 3) Finish pruning soft
fruit bushes by mid-March and give a high-nitrogen feed.4) New
shrubs and herbaceous plants can be planted when the conditions are
good. 5) Feed roses with a general fertiliser and do it again in
the summer.

April

1) Prune early-flowering shrubs such as Forsythia and Hamamelis as soon as flowering is over. 2) Continue to divide herbaceous plants if necessary. 3) Rake lawns to remove worm casts, twigs and old grass. 4) Trim lavenders to shape, but don't cut into the previous seasons wood. 5) Be sure to ventilate greenhouses and cold frames on warmer days.

May

1) Water any newly-planted trees & shrubs and give a general feed and a mulch to preserve water. 2) Clip established privet, ivy, lonicera. Also clip topiary to maintain a tidy appearance. 3) Keep weeds down by frequent hoeing, a 10cm mulch, or chemical sprays against perennial weeds. 4) Watch out for vivid red lily beetles from mid-May onwards, catch them and squash them! 5) Set lawn mower blades to their final height for summer. Apply a high-nitrogen fertiliser to the lawn.

June

1) Continue to stake and tie those tall plants which are still growing. 2) Deadhead roses after they have gone over, cut back to a leaf axil to promote new flower growth. 3) Keep cutting sweet peas to ensure repeat flowering. Kill greenfly as you do it! 4) Water containers whenever compost feels dry, add a liquid feed if no long-release feed was added. 5) Trim back the growth of Erica carnea varieties and top-dress with ericaceous compost.

July

1) When weather is very dry, give newly-planted trees a good soaking (better than little & often) 2) Clip large-leafed evergreen hedges this month using secateurs. Ensure there are no nesting birds. 3) Check the moisture level of hanging baskets every morning. Water thoroughly if dry & feed weekly. 4) Keep hydrangeas well-watered: they are quick to show the wilting signs of water shortage. 5) Prune pyracanthas by cutting side-shoots to 2-3 leaves from their base for a good show of berries.

August

1) Complete lifting of last season's bulbs and dry them off in woven sacks for maximum ventilation. 2) Clean up and dispose of early fallen fruit such as apples, to prevent disease spread. 3) Cut back long whippy growths of wisteria to within three buds of the old wood for maximum flowers. 4) Towards the end of the month cut back fruited canes of raspberries and tie in young shoots. 5) Keep hardy & half-hardy annuals well-watered and weed-free. Try not to walk on the growing beds.

September

1) Dig over the borders as bedding plants are removed later this month if you have heavy soil. 2) On a beautiful evening walk around the garden and make notes of all the things to improve for next year. 3) As lawn mowing diminishes, remove the old 'thatch' with a spring tine rake. Aerate with the prongs of a garden fork. 4) A good time to sort out and place your order for bulbs, plant tulips in November to reduce disease. 5) Crocosmias form large mounds of corms: divide with two forks, clean with a hose and replant.

October

1) Lift Dahlias and other tender perennials when temperatures fall sharply. Store in a frost-free place. 2) Collect seed of plants. Store dry seed in paper envelopes in the fridge bottom. 3) Collect leaves as they fall around the garden and store in a wire mesh bin for next years' compost. 4) Lift, divide, and replant rhubarb crowns which have been in the ground for at least five years. 5) An excellent month to lay turf on prepared, firm, weed-free and raked ground.

November

1) Be sure to check for hibernating animals (particularly hedgehogs) before lighting the bonfire. 2) Collect all stakes used for support around the garden, clean off. 3) Plant winter bedding such as wallflowers, pansies, primroses. 4) Start Amaryllis (Hippeastrum) bulbs for Christmas. 5) Place grease-bands on the trunks of fruit trees to catch female winter moths as they climb the tree.

December

1) To prevent flooding, ensure that rainwater drains on the property are not choked with leaves. 2) Make sure that all outside water taps and pipes are turned off and lagged. 3) Prune Acers and Betula sp. before mid-December to prevent wounds from bleeding. 4) Do not prune hamamelis or forsythia until after flowering. 5) Clean tools and sharpen.

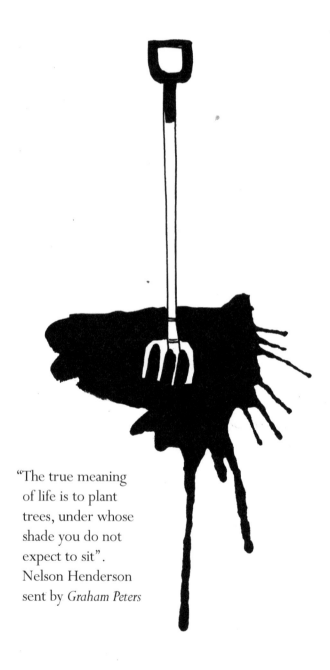

"The true meaning
 of life is to plant
 trees, under whose
 shade you do not
 expect to sit".
Nelson Henderson
sent by *Graham Peters*